JAZZ DRUMMING PERSPECTIVES

PETER ERSKINE

EDITED BY
RICK MATTINGLY

PLAYBACK+
Speed • Pitch • Balance • Loop

To access audio and video, visit:
www.halleonard.com/mylibrary

Enter Code
5951-5514-4662-1866

Front cover photo by Marco Glaviano

Audio tracks recorded at Puck Productions, Santa Monica, California (Aaron Walk, Engineer) and TriTone Studios, Glendale, California (Talley Sherwood, Engineer)

All play-along tracks courtesy of Fuzzy Music, LLC

ISBN 978-1-7051-8236-9

Visit Hal Leonard Online at
www.halleonard.com

World headquarters, contact:
Hal Leonard
7777 West Bluemound Road
Milwaukee, WI 53213
Email: info@halleonard.com

In Europe, contact:
Hal Leonard Europe Limited
Dettingen Way
Bury St Edmunds, Suffolk, IP33 3YB
Email: info@halleonardeurope.com

In Australia, contact:
Hal Leonard Australia Pty. Ltd.
4 Lentara Court
Cheltenham, Victoria, 3192 Australia
Email: info@halleonard.com.au

ACKNOWLEDGMENTS

I would like to thank you for reading this book, contemplating some of its ideas, and listening to my music.

I'd also like to thank everyone involved with the production of my original book *The Drum Perspective*, especially my editor Rick Mattingly.

Plus, I'd like to thank:

> drummer Alex Cline and correspondent Tom Moss for their insights;
>
> my other drumming colleagues and musical friends who have all contributed to my experience and knowledge in these matters over the years;
>
> all of the folks at Hal Leonard for their diligence and patience;
>
> Marco Glaviano for the use of his portrait of me on the front cover;
>
> Aaron Walk for his engineering excellence and assistance;
>
> Shawn Girsberger for her technical assistance;
>
> Steve Fidyk for his transcriptions, with honorable mention to Duncan Moore;
>
> the people at *Percussive Notes* and *Modern Drummer* magazines for suggesting and inspiring many of these writings;
>
> my father, Fred Erskine, M.D., for his proofreading and advice;
>
> and all of the record companies who so generously allowed me to use portions of their recordings that appear on the audio tracks that accompany this book.

Thanks to the wonderful artisans and generous businesspersons at the musical instrument companies whose instruments and support I have enjoyed over the years.

And, as always, the biggest thanks of all go to my wife Mutsy and children Taichi and Maya, who have taught me more about life and drumming than all the gigs and drum books in this world put together.

This book is dedicated to the memory of Don Grolnick: a master musician and composer, humorist, philosopher, and friend.

Ironically, I found the following during a morning's walk while doing a tour of the UK with Don in January, 1995. I chanced upon this epitaph in the church of St. Mary Redcliffe, Bristol, England, written for one Ralph Thompson Morgan (1876–1949, church organist 1906–1949), and felt compelled to copy the words down. Sadly, that tour turned out to be Don's final jazz concert tour (Don passed away in June, 1996). These words are as nice a way as any man might want to be remembered...

"Faithful in Service • Loving in Friendship

Skilled in Music • Happy in Life"

TABLE OF CONTENTS

INTRODUCTION

Ask eight drummers to play the same beat. Mechanically, it might not be that difficult for all of them to play it. But out of those eight, perhaps only one or two would play it in such a way that you would go, "Yeah!"

Why are some musicians so compelling when they play and others are not? Drumming is an interesting occupation in that regard because many people can do the job—play the downbeat, play the backbeat, play a fill, read all the figures, do what they are supposed to do. It's comparable to, "The car came down the assembly line, I bolted on the door, did everything I was supposed to do." That's fine; a person could work happily that way for years. But in music, a fine line distinguishes an inspired piece of music-making from something that's just OK or that might even stink, even though the person is putting the same effort or conscientiousness into it.

I recently discovered a "new" recording of Beethoven's Fifth Symphony. The conducting (by Carlos Kleiber) was so inspired, it was as if I were hearing that piece of music for the first time. Exhilarating! What was the difference between his and others' versions? Certainly, it was more than just Kleiber's technique or the choice of tempos and dynamics; there was something else, too. But if I had to choose two words to describe it, I would say it was its sense of "clarity" and "velocity." (The members of the Berlin Philharmonic might not agree with those word choices, but as a listener, that's what I felt.)

A beginner has to try out lots of things; you don't want to restrict your options. But for me, the last several years has been a reductive process of stripping away a lot of things and arriving at clarity and focus in my playing, and also as a way to hear music. After a certain point, I feel that I can listen to music and see right into its heart. I can tell rather quickly what a piece of music means to me and know if I want to invest much time listening to it (or playing it, though I do try to keep an open mind).

With certain players, you are drawn in and want to listen to every note and every new event. What's the difference that makes one person's playing sound good while another's is indistinguishable from a bunch of others? Is it a gift from God? Maybe that's a bigger question than we need to get into in this book. But I believe that if someone attempts to understand the mechanics of playing and the nature of space between notes, then it's possible for anyone to play something that is very inspiring to listen to.

Obviously, this inspiration comes not from just sitting and practicing for hours on end but from gaining insights and understanding of music. Some people naturally have some of these qualities. But reaching a more profound performance ability on your instrument comes from having listened to enough music to be able to draw from those examples and that inspiration, and be able to apply that.

If you're going to play funky music, certainly it would be important to listen to a lot of P-Funk, James Brown, or Sly and the Family Stone. But what happens when you also listen to Beethoven, Mozart, and Bach, and then you listen to Varése, Stravinsky, and Bartók, then to Charlie Parker, John Coltrane, and Miles Davis? As Dave Liebman pointed out, Miles could play a C# over a C major triad and it would sound great—the spacing, the timing, the conviction. With anyone else, it would sound like a mistake. So what makes Miles a "Miles?"

There's no guarantee that any musician—no matter how much he or she studies or thinks about the "correct things"—is going to produce a piece of music that people will be compelled to listen to. But certainly, a drummer who doesn't have a decent beat isn't going to get very far, unless the person is so completely inspired in some other area.

What you play must be believable and have a specific intent. Imagine an actor making an entrance on the stage and reciting a line. Who is this person? Why is he saying this? What's the motivation? It has to be believable, or it doesn't resonate.

On the other hand, there is the art of surrendering to the music, which to me implies relaxing the shoulders, breathing deeply, and giving yourself over to the flow of the music. You can certainly help determine that flow, but you're not imposing too much of your agenda on the proceedings. I have found that the concept of surrendering, which gets into the area of ego, helps me be that much more specific in my placement. But by specific I certainly don't mean overbearing.

Where is that balance?

Perhaps the yin/yang symbol is helpful here.

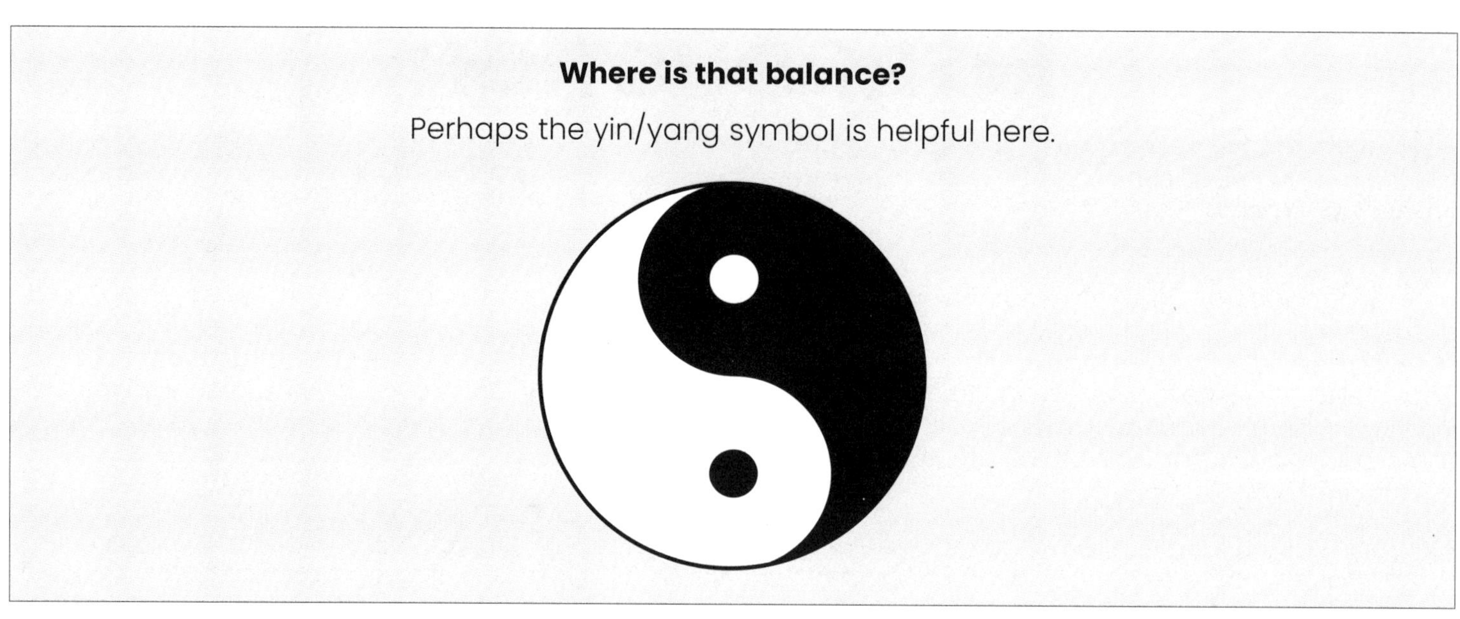

By surrendering, you become all-powerful. It's not passive, like, "I'll just go where the music takes me." It's surrendering your ego. I can play with incredible authority by playing softer and very simple. The drums rule at the moment; that's the beacon. Whether people know it or not doesn't matter. Sonically, you might have to do certain things in specific contexts; if you're in a big band, you have to take control, but it's a matter of, "This needs to happen for the music." It becomes easier to play with authority when you don't play from panic. If you're playing your instrument as though you're chewing your leg off to get out of a trap, you've really jeopardized your chances of sounding good. So it's like you've tapped into a higher awareness.

It's a very respectful way of treating the music, and it's very serious—although you can enjoy it and laugh, too. I take my playing very seriously, but I know it's not brain surgery. It's not life and death—and yet it is!

There are two orbits of discussion here that very much fit together, but they are paradoxes. You should aspire to freedom, and yet you need discipline and structure to make this happen.

The Japanese word or concept for harmony is "wa," which is the reconciling of the spiritual and physical. That could be related to the idea of expressing yourself as opposed to playing that which must be expressed—saying what you want to say as opposed to saying that which simply must be said—or left unsaid.

The idea behind this book is to combine the spiritual or philosophical approach to music and drumming with the physical or "mechanical" aspects of what we do. Every point of discussion we have about playing the instrument, on whatever idealistic or aesthetic level, can be explained on a very basic, mechanical level. Philosophies of drumming are not just flights of fancy. For every aesthetic ideal that you can suggest or ponder, there is a mechanical reality that corresponds to it. It's not a duality; it's a real partnership.

NOTATION KEY

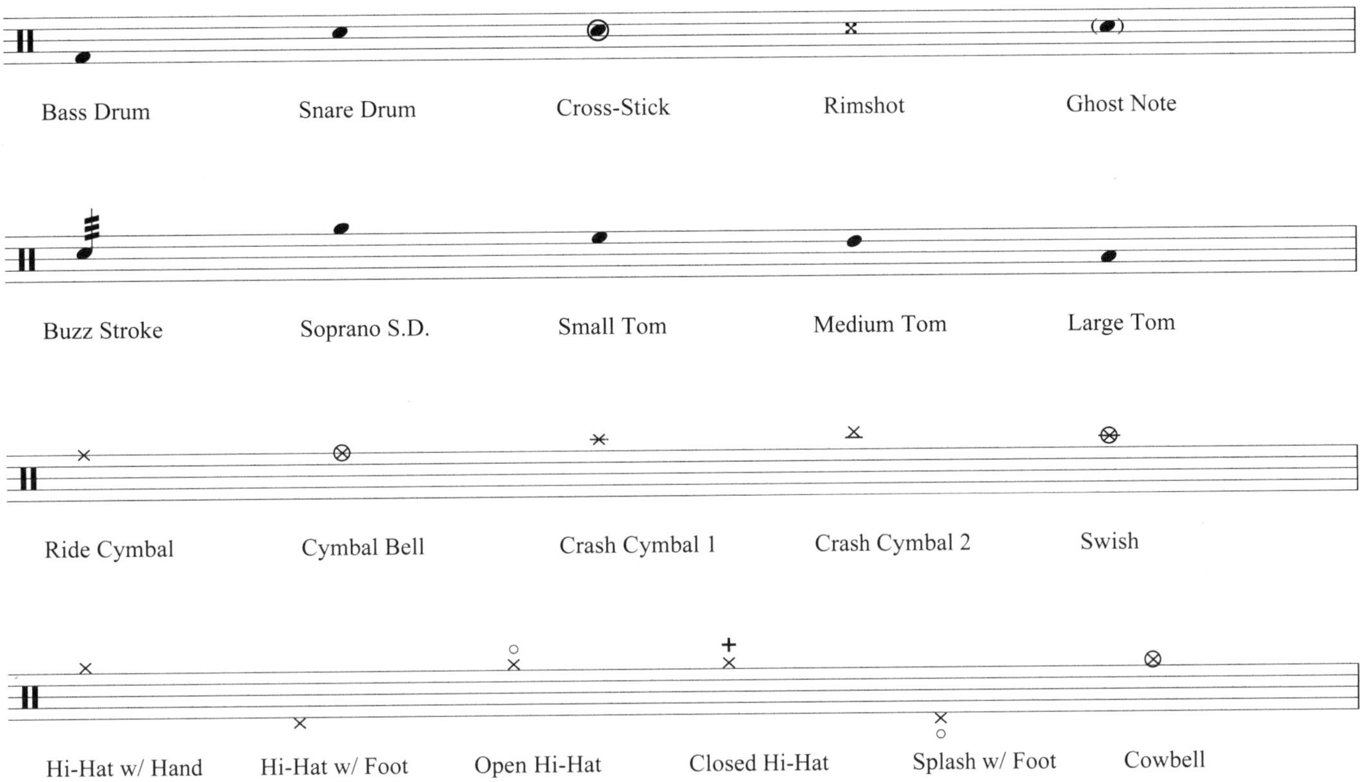

CHAPTER 1
YOUR RELATIONSHIP TO THE DRUMS

> *"All of the drummers from that era—from Jo Jones right through to Elvin Jones—played with such lovely lifts, and their feet would be going like they were bicycling. It all comes from the arse, you know. It's lovely to see."*
>
> —Charlie Watts

If you say so, Charlie!

While I was a student at Indiana University, Mstislav Rostropovitch came to the campus and gave a cello recital that was magnificent. Every note he played exuded a tremendous amount of passion, warmth, and humanity (not to mention good intonation!).

But the best and most memorable part of the concert for me was at the very beginning, when he strode onto the stage. Following his accompanist, Rostropovitch walked briskly across the large stage with his cello, acknowledging the audience's applause. No sooner had he plopped himself down onto his chair than he immediately began to play—brilliantly! It was obvious that he was one with his instrument. There was no unnecessary motion or maneuvering on his part to get adjusted to his instrument or comfortable with the fact that he was about to play. The cello was a part of him, and he was a part of it. Both parts made the whole.

Do we regard the drumset and ourselves in the same manner?

The best way to establish rapport with something, or someone, is to spend time with that object or person—the more time the better. Whether it be friend or instrument (some people's instruments are their best friends!), you want to feel as natural and comfortable as possible; you want to feel that you can just "be yourself." Applying that idea specifically to the drumset, let's look at your physical and musical relationship with the drums, starting with the way you play them.

Grip and Stroke

Whatever grip you choose to use, traditional or matched, it's important that you have a firm enough grasp of the stick that it doesn't fly out of your hands. It's important to play as relaxed as possible, and utilizing the fulcrum point of the stick will provide the most efficient means of playing the instrument.

For many years, I was holding the sticks a little too far back. This might have been a natural reaction to playing louder music earlier in my life. A lot of us resorted to holding the sticks a little further back, figuring we'd get that much more power. But that takes away from the ability of the stick to rebound, so you have to work harder.

An interesting thing I have noticed recently is that I appear to "guide" the sticks more as opposed to "holding" them. Could this be a realization of my getting closer to some sort of player/instrument ideal?

My grip and stroke will change to allow me to remain as centered as possible—particularly when it's just for single notes on different parts of the kit. I don't change my body's center of gravity or approach to the kit. I sit relaxed and centered, and I will pivot my wrist to strike a cymbal off to my right or to travel between the toms so that the arm movement is minimized.

Make sure your arms are always relaxed. Let them hang down by your side naturally—not far away from your body or tightly against it. Depending on your body size and shoulder width, your elbows may or may not be touching your torso. Then, bring your forearms up so that the elbows are at an approximately 90-degree angle, without moving the elbows towards or away from your body. And, if your elbows DO touch your body when relaxed, then they should remain touching your torso unless you really need to reach for something.

Some people have noticed that I play almost backhanded sometimes, which I guess isn't really great technique, per se, but it makes it easier for me to get around the kit. I try to keep my drum setup economical so I don't have to reach too far or reset myself to strike any part of the instrument.

With some drummers, you'll often see their whole torso turn to play a short series of notes around the kit when it's not really necessary. The arms and wrists can do a lot of that traveling. You shouldn't need to change your entire body position to move around on the kit.

An important aspect of the stroke is maintaining a consistent rebound, which means that you're always in position to play. You are able to make any stroke for any rhythm you want to play, as opposed to having the sticks up in the air. I've noticed that no matter how much time I have between notes, by focusing and keeping my stick in position, my placement is much improved.

Tone

I've worked for many years on lightening up my touch while attempting to get a fuller sound out of the drums and cymbals. I've found this next concept to be very important in helping me achieve that.

Trained pianists draw tone out of their instrument by letting their arms fall a little below the keyboard. This gravity and weight produces a fuller tone than if they were just playing from above the keys with wrists and fingers.

My touch on the instrument is akin to that technique. It's not that I'm trying to play beneath the surface of the instrument, as do many drummers who are basically having collisions with their drums and cymbals. Freddie Gruber once started tap dancing for me and said, "See, I'm not trying to dance beneath the surface of the floor. I'm dancing on top of it." Then, he would sit down at the drums and sort of do the same thing with his hands. It was the whole idea that you can't beat sound into the drums; it has to be pulled *out* of the instrument.

When Joe Zawinul used to sit down at my drumset during Weather Report soundchecks, he would say, "You know, on this tune I think the beat should be more like this." It didn't matter whether it was a fast tune, a slow tune, swing feel, straight eighth or sixteenth feel; whatever it was, he would always play the same "boogie-woogie" kind of beat. It finally dawned on me that what he was trying to convey was an element of dancing. He wanted the beat to dance, and what he played on the drums did have a dancing quality.

When you dance, you can't try to step though the floor or you'll look like Frankenstein. Compare that to the way Gene Kelly or Fred Astaire danced; it was light. Buddy Rich had that quality in his drumming, and so did Louie Bellson. It sparkles because they were drawing the tone out of the instrument.

So the execution can be lightly rendered, but the weight of the arm is contributing to the fullness of the tone. You're getting more resonance out of the instrument without having to dig in too deeply.

This goes with the whole idea of the center of the drumming stroke being at the core of the drummer himself or herself. I see a lot of players externalize the whole process in their forearms; they're playing the instrument from above rather than from deeply within.

The best exercise I can think of to develop that is to play long tones on the drums and cymbals, concentrating on the basics of rebound and tone. Then, play very slow pulses—maybe half notes at a particular tempo—so that you can discover your touch on the instrument. Pay attention to how parallel the stick or brush is in relation to the drumhead or cymbal; the more parallel you are to the instrument, the fuller your sound will be.

Ultimately, developing "touch" is the result of both playing and listening experience.

And, ultimately, TONE is a huge component of the way that music swings and feels.

Some Thoughts:

Don't over-prepare your stroke. Play direct.

Your touch has to always be available (from loud gig to soft).

To my ears, if the tip of the drumstick is too big, you do not get the true sound of a cymbal; it's mostly attack.

Playing relaxed is not the same as playing sloppy.

Please Listen Carefully

Drummers are known by the skill of their hands (and feet). But any musician's most important asset is his or her hearing. The ability to hear clearly informs our musical choices and allows us to enjoy the results of our own work or another's efforts—like Mozart's or Steve Gadd's. But what can happen if we take our hearing for granted? The possibilities include hearing loss and a condition called **tinnitus**.

I've lost some of my hearing, and I have tinnitus (pronounced by my doctor with the accent on the first syllable, soft "i" in the second). In simple terms, tinnitus is a constant ringing in the ears. It doesn't go away. It can be loud and distressing. It affects many musician friends of mine.

My ears used to ring a lot after performances, especially when I was working with big bands or groups with electronic instruments. At the time, I was more bemused than alarmed by this ringing because it would be gone by the next morning, and I could think, "Man, that was *loud*!"

But one day, it didn't go away.

I was aware of my progressive hearing loss and charted it by visiting an ear doctor semi-annually, but I didn't know the fate I was courting. Now, fortunately, there is a heightened awareness about hearing trauma and loss.

Loud music can damage your hearing. Drums are especially dangerous! PROTECT YOUR HEARING. Wear earplugs if necessary, rest your ears whenever possible, be wary of monitor cabinets and headphones (and rimshots!), and educate those around you.

For live concerts, I now prefer to have no monitor whenever possible in order to keep the stage volume soft. For me, the best music is made that way. That said, there are now numerous options, most of them excellent, for in-ear monitoring. As with anything regarding your hearing, please exercise the greatest care possible not to damage your ears. While some drummers will use protective hearing headsets or earplugs for practicing, I am of the mind and conviction that proper practicing need not be loud. It is much harder to discern the tone you are creating when you are hitting the drum much harder than necessary.

I don't intend to paint an entirely bleak picture, particularly for those who already suffer from this malaise. I have noticed that whenever my ears are rested, the condition can improve temporarily. Stress and the amount of physical exercise you get may also play a part in the severity of the symptoms. Obviously, less stress and more exercise are good ideas for anyone to follow. Research is now underway toward greater understanding and possible treatment.

You should visit an ear doctor on a regular basis, and I certainly suggest that you seek further information about hearing damage and loss.

It may be a coincidence, but I find that I enjoy softer music more nowadays—just for the pure aesthetics of it. Drums and cymbals can have such a wonderful tone when their sound is drawn out, rather than pounded in. The same goes for all instruments. And while I like a good *fortissimo* as much as the next person, I've come to appreciate the beauty of a well-played whisper.

Anyway, as the beboppers used to say: "Straight ahead and strive for tone."

Musical Relationship to the Drums

I'm a terrible one for analogies, so I ask your indulgence and, perhaps, forgiveness if I say that playing the drums should be as natural as sitting down and eating a sandwich! Whether you eat with your elbows on or off the table, you still just wrap your hands around the sandwich and take a bite. Simple as that. And that's how it should be when you sit down to play the drums.

In other words, *it should not be a big deal.* Assuming that you spend a good portion of your time at the kit, and further, assuming that you spend a good deal of that time *playing time*, then all you should have to do is to draw on that experience, give yourself an upbeat, and boom—away you go! You should be prepared to play any beat and any tempo (within reason) on the drums. If this is what we do, then let's do it!

I had a student come for a lesson who played a lot of rock but wanted to work on his jazz stuff. So he sat down behind the kit, and when he played, there was a lot of extra movement, like his idea of some sort of jazz attitude. His body was angled, and there wasn't a direct focus to what he was playing; there was too much stick movement and extraneous motion. There was no center to the sound.

I asked him to play one of the rock songs that his band did, and it was very direct, relaxed, centered. He was sitting there like it was the most natural thing in the world. I asked him to play another jazz thing, and immediately his posture got weird and curved over, and even his face was making these "cool" jazz gestures. So I told him, "Excuse me for saying this, but it's as if you're putting on a beret and sunglasses. You're not playing the music; it's more like you're play-acting. Bring the same directness of approach to jazz that you bring to rock."

A fair amount of artifice can get injected into music. You see people who start to play and their upper lip curls into a snarl. I see some classical pianists make grand gestures and bring their hands way up. Does that help or does it get in the way? A certain amount of "show-biz" is OK; you want the audience to be able to see what you're doing. But when we do something, it's best that we do it in the most natural way. I find there is a lot of conflicting body energy and motion used by many musicians, and it is as apt to show up in free music as any other.

I really had to learn to relax. One of the most practical things I can think to mention is the importance of breathing deeply. I recall a situation in which I hated the music I was being asked to play. My wife came up to me afterwards and said that I didn't look very comfortable. I asked her how she could tell, and she said I was only breathing from my upper chest. When you're relaxed, you breathe deeply. That oxygen is vital. When you constrict, there is no flow. I had to consciously become aware of my breathing. (This was also the point in my musical development when I began to learn about the art of surrendering to the music and accepting the circumstances under which I was playing.)

When I was in Weather Report, Joe Zawinul once told me, "You know, man, you played a beat tonight that didn't sound right, and when I turned around and looked at you, man, it didn't look right neither." I had my shoulders all hunched up. I went back to my hotel room that evening, sat in front of the mirror, and compared the relaxed versus non-relaxed way of sitting at the (imaginary) drumset. Sometimes you need feedback—like a mirror, or a video or audio playback (or a teacher or bandleader!)—to become aware of certain things you're doing.

All of this being said, however, I don't mean to suggest that your music-making become a completely cerebral affair. It's also good to get excited about the music and to allow your emotions, as expressed through physical movement, to come through. Recently, long-time friend (and excellent drummer) Steve Smith commented to me after a particularly energetic performance of mine: "I like it when you get excited!" Our old friend, the yin-yang symbol, representing balance in all things, comes to mind once more.

In any event, let's strive to be as natural and well-acquainted with our instrument as Mr. Rostropovitch. Were it as easily done as said!

Warming Up

Vic Firth counseled me some years ago that warming up would become more and more necessary as I aged. And though I have indeed grown older, my go-to warm-up exercise is the same routine that was first shown to me over 50 years ago by Professor George Gaber. Beginning with the right hand, I play eight strokes, followed by eight strokes with the left; then seven (R), seven (L), six (R), six (L), five (R), five (L), and so on. It looks like this:

8	7	6	5	4	3	2	1	2	3	4	5	6	7	8
R↓	R↓	R↓	R↓	R↓	R↓	R↓	R↓	R↓	R↓	R↓	R↓	R↓	R↓	R↓
L↗	L↗	L↗	L↗	L↗	L↗	L↗	L↗	L↗	L↗	L↗	L↗	L↗	L↗	L

The warm-up can be played either unaccented or with an accent at the beginning of each hand's new sequence. You can also play these in unison (without flams).

I've played this exercise dutifully over the years but never so mindfully as I do now—or as *soft* as I do now. You see, this warm-up is like a communion and benediction for me. This approach was inspired by learning the following about the late, great cellist Pablo Casals (1876–1973): "Casals attributes his long life and youthfulness to his habit of playing Bach's Preludes and Fugues on the piano every morning. This communion with a great mind renews his spirit and creates in him a cheerful mood with which to begin the day's work. 'Each day I am born anew,' he says." [*The Guardian*] OK, so "8–7–6–5–4–etc." is not Bach, but I treat this mechanical exercise in much the same way. How so?

I find music in these repetitions by concentrating on the tone my sticks are making on a practice pad (yes!). And the best way to do this, I have found, is to limit the rebound height as well as the velocity of the sticks and the speed of the strokes. Fast and loud are NOT the goals here; quite the contrary: I am using this moment to say "hello" to my hands, fingers, elbows, back, ears, mind, sticks, the pad, room, and life itself. 8–7–6–5–4–3–2–1 and back again.

And then, I migrate to improvised singles and doubles on the pad, always paying attention to stick heights, rebound angles, and sound. After that, I move to playing eighth notes on the kit, softly and slowly, or at a medium tempo (I would recommend no faster than quarter note = 160 BPM).

I *listen* to my playing as I play these simple repetitions, trying different tempos and different volumes. Do any of the rhythms sound or feel out of place? If so, then that's our music ecosystem telling us what needs work. Improvising my way around the kit is my favorite way to go, but for those who enjoy a bit of rigor, try the following exercises: single (alternate) stickings as well as doubles or random combinations of singles/doubles, accented, unaccented, or randomly accented. Try what works best, as well as what *doesn't* work best, and learn to recognize the difference.

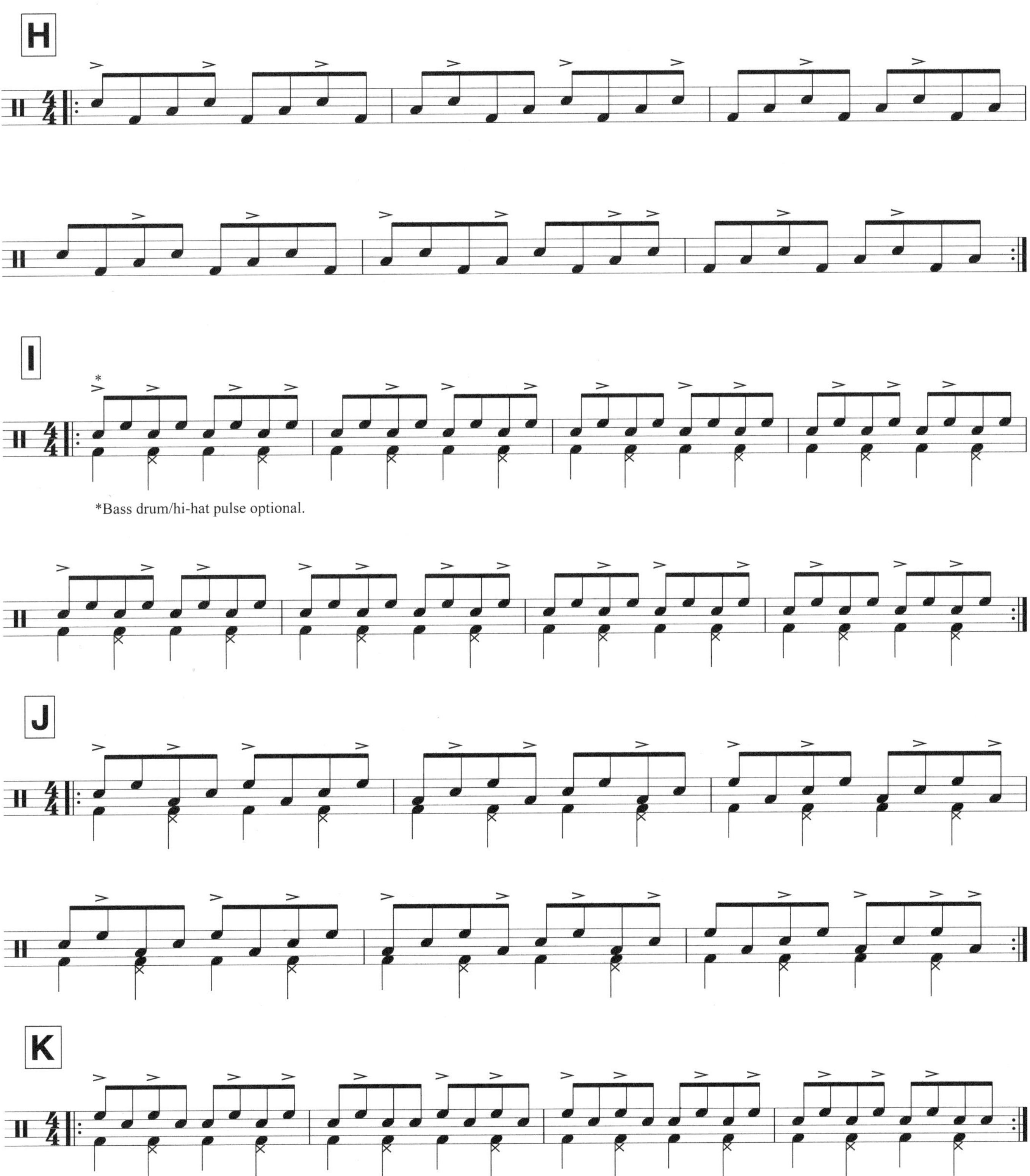
H
I
*Bass drum/hi-hat pulse optional.
J
K

CHAPTER 2
FUNCTION OF THE DRUMS

> *"There is nothing to it. You only have to hit the right note at the right time, and the instrument plays itself."*
>
> —Johann Sebastian Bach

Pulse and Subdivisions

Life is full of choices, and so is music. We should always try to make the best choices. In life, that would be determined, in large part, by our cultural and religious heritage and what our parents teach us, as well as by our society (government) and its laws. In music, the style and setting of a particular music will suggest certain possibilities. The bottom line in life, I believe, is to act responsibly and with respect for others. The bottom line in music is that it should *sound* good.

I often ask clinic audiences, "What is the job of a drummer?" Answers come back such as, "Play a groove." "Keep time." "Make the music feel good." OK, fine. What does that mean?

We make the music feel good by our timekeeping.

The quarter-note pulse is the most basic rhythmic element in contemporary music. It's crucial to also have an understanding and appreciation of how vital the subdivisions are within that pulse. The subdivisions define the style of a piece of music. So if you want to play any music authentically, you must know the **subdivision**. That's the "feel."

For example, jazz music primarily relies on the quarter-note pulse for its forward motion, usually supplied by the "walking" bass line. The quarter-note pulse is the driving force. The swung eighth note, or triplet feel, is the subdivision and the prominent rhythmic characteristic of jazz.

I phrase the above with an emphasis on each quarter note. It's not so much a matter of toning down on beats 2 and 4, but rather driving towards beats 1 and 3. This is for clarity's sake.

A very interesting example is when you play the most basic of jazz rhythms: four quarter notes on the ride cymbal, hi-hat on 2 and 4, and a cross-stick on every fourth beat, like classic Jimmy Cobb on "Freddie Freeloader" (from *Kind of Blue* by Miles Davis).

2

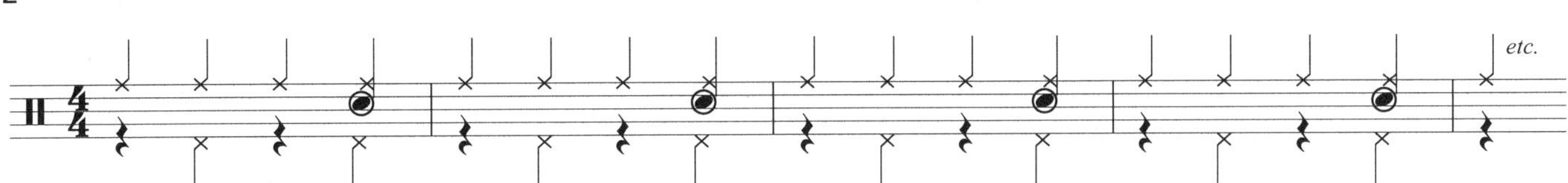

Mechanically and coordination-wise, any drummer who can hold a pair of drumsticks can play that. Now, if I'm just thinking quarter notes, it comes out stiff with no personality and no swing. But if I'm thinking of the triplet subdivision, which that style of music is based on, the difference is profound in how it sounds—even if I'm not playing the subdivision at that moment. The spaces between the notes have meaning and the note placement swings. It's a subtle yet important difference. I am honoring and carving out the spaces between the notes.

Please refer to Track 37, "Pedagogical," on the accompanying audio files and see my comments on that track in Chapter 17.

In pop, rock, or funk music, the subdivision is more of a "straight" eighth- or sixteenth-note feel.

In order to groove, there has to be accurate placement of the beat—not only the pulse, but also the smallest denominator of the subdivision. You have to be aware of that, singing it to yourself as you're playing. If I'm thinking of eighth notes when I'm playing a straight eighth-note beat, it's virtually impossible for my bass drum, snare drum, hi-hat, or any part of a fill to be played in the wrong place, to be out of tempo, to be out of meter, or out of the groove.

If you play purely from muscle memory, then it's possible—and likely—that your drumming is not going to swing or groove and that the placement is going to be inaccurate. A good example is an eighth-note groove with occasional sixteenth-note bass drum figures.

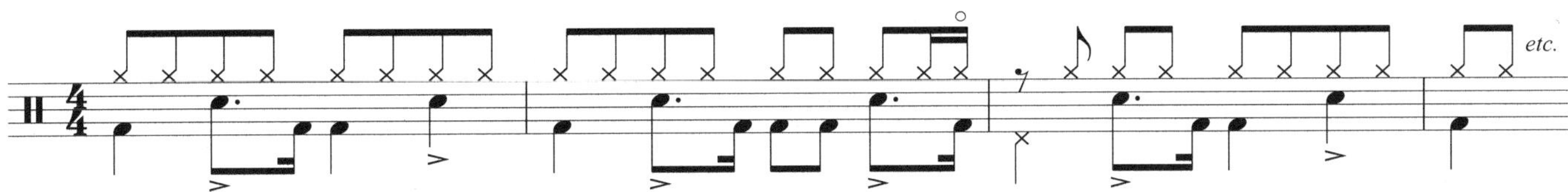

Even though I'm not playing sixteenth notes all the time on hi-hat, the fact that I'm playing *any* sixteenth notes means that I should be singing that subdivision. Otherwise, it's just my ankle that's going to try to put the notes where they're supposed to be instead of my entire musical being.

When I (subconsciously) sing the subdivisions to myself, I've established an internal reference point, and everything that I play will relate and lock onto that groove. When I sing to myself, I am not counting the subdivisions ("1-e-&-a, 2-e-&-a," etc.), but rather singing an appropriate-feeling rhythm part (like, for example, a rhythm guitar part). Of course, it is necessary to listen to the rest of the rhythm section in order to be able to play any kind of beat together!

Having a reference point really helps me in my realization of any kind of a beat or performance, whether I'm playing free, playing traditional swing, or playing rhythm 'n' blues. If I tune into the subdivision of the song, everything else just falls into place.

I discovered something interesting when I was working with singer Boz Scaggs. I was, of course, trying to play a lot of the beats that Jeff Porcaro played on Boz's records, and I was doing a pretty good imitation of Jeff. But I realized, especially playing alongside percussionist Lenny Castro, that I was playing on the surface of the music. At some point, there was a subtle transformation, and I started playing from within as I began to understand why, for example, Jeff played a particular fill and how it really functioned within the beat. I was then able to play it more as part of the beat structure as opposed to a fill on the top. And when the subtle mind shift occurred, out of the corner of my eye I saw Lenny look over and smile because then it felt authentic.

What was the difference? One was merely imitative and the other involved organically playing the fill as part of the music. What makes it one or the other? I believe that the difference comes from the immersion into the subdivision so that your whole being is there playing it. It's very believable, very specific. The spaces between the notes are exactly what they should be, and that comes from a stronger identification with the subdivision.

So in meeting a piece of music for the first time, you have to be aware of what kind of subdivision the music requires. At more advanced levels of music making, this can be like shifting sands. You can change subdivisions all over the place, and a lot of the more interesting improvising ensembles will do that. But doing that successfully only comes from the experience of being able to play in different rhythmic contexts.

Even though you are singing the smallest subdivisions to yourself, your playing can still have elasticity. The subdivisions in your mind are simply the reference point. Even when I'm playing fairly loose, it's not rhythmic guesswork. It's pretty close to the pocket. That's a very fine line.

The experience of playing basic beats really well in a variety of styles allows you to play at the tempo extremes, fast or slow, because you've established a reference point of what it's supposed to feel like.

When you're playing at a fast tempo, even though you can't subdivide that quickly because it's going by so fast, you know how the beats should connect—the quarter-note pulse and the eighth-note subdivisions, or whatever. So when you speed it up, you know what it feels like to swing at this tempo. As you move up the tempo scale, you're drawing on that, even though you aren't singing the subdivisions so much. There's no contradiction when I say, "Think slow when you're playing fast." Enjoy the scenery and try to see the bigger picture.

The inverse of that idea can apply when you're playing slow, except now you might be thinking fast. You have more time to sing subdivisions, so even though you're not necessarily playing sixteenth or thirty-second notes, you can be singing some of those subdivisions in a medium tempo.

To play musically, we must respect each note to the fullest. In other words, do not cheat the beat. And by allowing room for each of your notes to "sing" and for the other instruments in the band to speak, some real dialogue and communication can happen on the bandstand—and to me, that's what contemporary music is all about.

Conceptually, one way I think of this is as real-time architecture with a three-dimensional idea of space and placement that provides depth, air, and light in the music as opposed to density. The reference points are vital; the issue is whether or not you fill them up with all these subdivisions when you're playing. One style of playing, which is the way I'm generally trying to play, leaves something to the listener's imagination. It invites the listener in.

It can be exciting, hip, and dramatic sounding to play very densely and fill up every subdivision. But if the playing on any instrument is too muscular, there's no room for the listeners to lean forward in their seats and enter into the dialogue. It's like in certain films where the director has a lot of patience and lets the actors take their time. That's a very satisfying kind of cinematic moment for me because I can enter in. It's rich with possibilities for the viewer, as opposed to an action film where you're assaulted with the velocity and imagery, and then it's over and you're not sure how you feel about it. There's a correlation there.

When I hear Paul Motian play, sometimes it's so open and a real surprise because I don't know whether he's going to hit an accent here or an accent there. It's a wonderfully organic blossoming of the music, and the listener can get emotionally involved. To me, that's a lot more interesting than the real dense stuff.

Whether or not something is interesting becomes an important aesthetic criterion. Something can be well-played, but if it's essentially vapid, then as well-crafted as some of it might be, it has the aesthetic quality of a greeting card—and that's not where you'll find any real poetry, even though the words might rhyme. Much of the current commercial jazz might sound good and be produced well. But in general, that music is either very dense with notes and ideas, and everybody is just doing their own thing and playing along with whatever kind of grooves, or it is created for the sole purpose of selling huge numbers of records. It's background music to I-don't-know-what, and it is not satisfying to listen to. Frankly speaking, I don't understand the current ethos of many people's aesthetics.

Fusion music had a lot of things "wrong" with it, specifically the barriers musicians put up between themselves and the other players. There was a fair degree of self-absorption in the quest to play more powerfully, and the "communication" (what there was of it) was often superficial. Also, the volume plus lack of dynamics was often a problem. But a lot of fusion music still sounds fresh to me (as do Beatles recordings), and it beats much of what I'm hearing nowadays in popular instrumental music. Much of that music was well-intentioned, as opposed to being contrived to sell a lot of records (even if a lot of the older jazz musicians at the time didn't dig it; Joe Zawinul was always caught between those two worlds when he would encounter old friends from his more straight-ahead jazz days). Of course, nowadays, who even buys records?

There's so much great music that is the living history of jazz; restricting one's diet of music to "wave"-type jazz is like subsisting on watching television sitcoms or eating a solely fast-food diet. Just spend two minutes thinking about that, and you'll realize that you're missing an awful lot by not exploring the music made by jazz's truly creative musicians.

It's regrettable that the arts are not supported in the United States to the extent they are in Europe. European radio and television regularly broadcast a whole evening's worth of specially composed new music. That is a rarity in the country where jazz was born! Oftentimes, the little snatches of quality music you can hear on the radio in the U.S. is sandwiched between musical efforts that sit on the other end of the artistic spectrum.

There will always be people who respond to simplistic artistic fare or shallow show-biz musical efforts. These musicians play, for the most part, from "without," not from "within." It's as if it is all for external effect—not expressing that which must be expressed, in my opinion. Besides, most of the "wave" radio-type players I've encountered on a professional basis (recording sessions) don't really consider themselves jazz musicians at all. The conversations I've overheard on at least two sessions I was involved with as a sideman went like this: "Hey, wow, this is like we're making a real jazz album!" It could be just because there's some element of actual improvisation going on, or maybe a couple of the chords happened to be "hip." If you haven't listened to any, say, Duke Ellington or Louis Armstrong in a while, you're denying yourself a tremendous amount.[1]

It is often a lot hipper to simplify. Trust yourself and trust the music so you don't stretch to the limits of your technical abilities when the tune is asking for something simpler. You'll want to impose a discipline on your choices in order to come to greater understanding of what the different elements can do. Practice playing only eighth notes—no double strokes, no rolls, no fancy licks. What can you play that is melodic, musical, and memorable, that works within very limited parameters? As Elvin Jones once said in a *Modern Drummer* interview, you can start with one snare and one tom-tom and right there you have infinite possibilities—which is vastly different from the type of drumming that involves a lot of notes and technique that is all over the place.

---

1 Pianist Keith Jarrett, responding to the question, "Are there sources or influences (re: his improvisational 'lines' being unique)?" in the January/February 1997 issue of *Piano & Keyboard* magazine, said: "Well, I'm not afraid to play what I've heard. In other words, one thing you're hearing is that I'm not worried about being me, so I can let things enter the music. Maybe some players would worry about their identity. If you let enough of those things enter, then it reverses; the coin flips over again and you become very much an identifiable player because you allow those things in. Gary (Peacock) said to me once, 'Every time the trio plays, it's like we are taking in more history each time.' It isn't like people will say I'm using so-and-so's licks. But if you let something enter, then there's a bunch more possibilities."

I played on a recording project for Pat Williams and his big band titled *Sinatraland*, featuring songs that had been recorded by Frank Sinatra. I tried to approach this music as myself, but I imagined myself an incarnation of Irv Cottler, Alvin Stoller, and Mel Lewis! That meant playing a lot of simple backbeats on 2 and 4 (with a combination rim/head hit) while playing the swung ride-cymbal pattern:

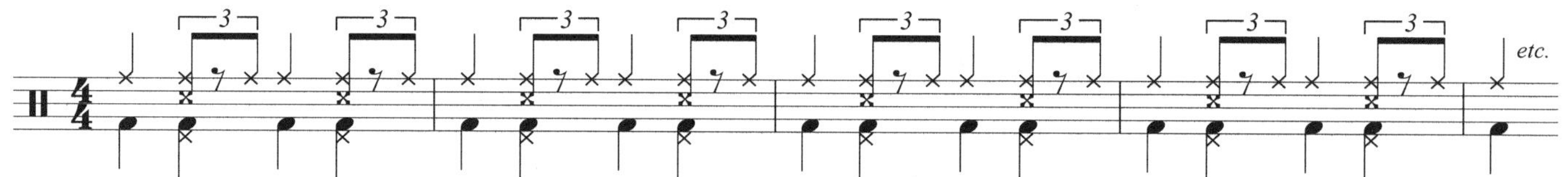

The sheer simplicity of the way drummers like Irv Cottler, Alvin Stoller, and Mel Lewis played was a tremendous part of their genius and good taste. The music simply swings more when you lay it down like that! (It also had to do with the fact the drums were often in the same room as the other instruments, and that those other instruments' microphones were also "hearing" the drums; too many notes resulted in too much sound or information.)

I'm always preaching simplicity, and on some of the things I play, there is simplicity and great clarity. But a lot of times, it can get fairly dense with a fair amount of activity. My position is that you are free to do whatever you are moved to do, and in my experience, it's much more successful if it ties into that reference point of very simple, very basic, very swinging timekeeping, and the ability to accurately place these on- and off-the-beat rhythms within a bar. So once you've passed that litmus test, you don't consciously plug in technical exercises you've learned from various method books, but instead, use them to start constructing the shape or the counterpoint, or to engage in the dialogue.

We're dealing with the micro-elements, which are the actual rhythms in each bar, and then the macro view is the larger pattern that emerges.

All of this is to urge you to consider getting the most out of your drumming with the least amount of strokes—to make each beat count for the fullest. And by establishing the timekeeping and feel with an "open" beat, your ears, and the music, are free to explore and develop any idea to its maximum (or minimum!) potential.

Which takes us back to listening. What is it that we're doing? Every time we play something, we don't have to pull out all our creative resources and inject them into the music. It's unfair to the music. It's imposing our agenda on the music as opposed to letting the music tell us what to do.

Once, while presenting a jazz drumming class at an east coast university, I was asked, "How has your drumming changed from when you were a younger player?" Hmmm. How best to answer? Should I provide some sort of specific assessment of my musical evolution? Perhaps a comparative analysis of my stylistic growth would suffice. Highlight the changes in my influences as my listening and perceptual horizons became broader? Or, maybe I could simply discuss what I do now as compared to what I didn't do when I was a young professional (or vice-versa).

My answer surprised me as it spontaneously formulated itself in my thoughts, and it was spoken aloud after only a moment's hesitation: "When I was younger, I played as though my life depended on it. Now, I play as though someone else's life depends on it."

CHAPTER 3

TIMEKEEPING

> *"If you're going to play good jazz you've got to have a plan of what's going to happen. There has to be intent. It's like an act of murder. You play with an intent to commit something."*
>
> —Duke Ellington

Drummers must understand whether they're using the drumset architecturally or compositionally in terms of outlining rhythmic shapes, as opposed to just using the drumset as a means of propelling the beat along.

For example, the snare drum can function as a specific snare voice or as part of the ride beat, in which case, it is fitting in dynamically with what the ride cymbal is playing and rhythmically helping propel it along. There is a fine line between playing the snare drum compositionally and playing the kind of repetitive patterns that a lot of drummers get into. I call that "doggy paddling," where a relatively limited vocabulary is constantly creeping into what the left hand is doing. The playing is not only redundant, but you also lose focus of what the ride cymbal is doing. ("Doggy paddling" refers to the way novice swimmers thrash about in the water, moving their arms and hands rapidly to stay afloat, much like a dog in water. Experienced swimmers trust the physics of buoyancy to stay afloat, freeing their arms and hands to make smooth motions that propel them forward.)

When there is an intent to your playing, there is a corresponding intensity. For me, everything is referenced to the ride cymbal. Everything I play with the left hand either assists the timekeeping or makes a definite statement rhythmically. So it's compositionally important—a deeper part of the tune. I'm not just ornamenting and playing along.

Another way to think about it: Try being *compositional* in your approach to timekeeping, as opposed to merely being reactive (or, be *proactive* instead of just being *reactive*).

Buddy Rich was constantly playing the snare drum and bass drum as part of the timekeeping. He was using the bass drum for offbeat rhythmic accents (not just on all four beats of the bar); it was a tap-dancing approach to playing, similar in a way to what Jack DeJohnette does, but different.

My private crusade for quite a few years has been to get away from the need to constantly be chugging along to make the music move. One's not right and one's not wrong; they're both very suitable. But it's worth noting the difference and being able to play in a more open manner, not only for aesthetic reasons, but because it allows drummers to discover how their time actually feels.

If you've got all your limbs going all the time, it might be swinging or it might not. You might not be able to tell because you're too busy just chugging along. So the reduction process has been crucial to me in learning the true essence of my beat. Then, if I want to play busier, I've got that reference point.

That's the basic principle—being able to just play "ding ding-a ding" and make it swing. That's how you're going to discover where your true beat is.

All of that being said... I've had the pleasure of hearing the great Billy Higgins play, and his drumming had all sorts of wonderful, constant commenting—truly conversational and compositional, in the bebop style. So the point of all of this is not to discourage polyrhythmic activity! Rather, I would encourage you to find the center of your beat, and then expand on that as the musical situation warrants or invites.

Swingin'

Swing is not so much a triplet feel; it's more of a legato thing. If we listen to a fast bebop line, like a Charlie Parker melody, it swings, right? But you'd be hard-pressed to find a triplet in there. Now think of the Lawrence Welk theme song; that was explicit triplets—and that ain't jazz; that's "Squaresville." So the phrasing becomes essential because what we're really doing is accenting the offbeat, and more importantly, the notes are connected in a legato sense. It's the legato phrasing that really makes something swing.

The ride cymbal pattern is going to be closer to a triplet: "ding, ding-a, ding, ding-a, ding." Here's where everything comes together in this beautiful full-circle moment. The rhythm is from Africa through the Afro-Caribbean portal where the "two" and the "three" start to rub, and that rub is what swings. So the "two/three" interrelationship is the mystery, the thrill, the excitement, the beauty of this music. It's what makes anything feel great. That gets us into the areas of intention: how we are conceiving of the music, and then what's played and what isn't played.

I have my students play melodies just on the snare drum, either with brushes or sticks, and make it swing—oftentimes reducing it to one hand on the hi-hat. If you can swing a band with one hand on the hi-hat or with just brushes on the snare drum, you can swing. That takes me back years ago, seeing Jeff Hamilton. The music was swinging like crazy, and Jeff was just playing on a snare drum. We're the same age; we went to college together, but I remember thinking, "I want to be able to do that when I grow up." I could see that this was a very mature way of playing.

Here is an example of a bouncing bebop melody played on the snare drum. The notes suggested or assigned to the right hand are, generally, of a higher pitch in the melodic shape (just as horn players will use more of their diaphragm and air power to produce these higher notes, the dominant hand can more easily accomplish the contours of the melody by giving varied emphasis to match the melody), while the "diddles" or double stickings in the left hand provide a more legato rendering than alternate sticking might otherwise produce.

Now, try this on your own: Find a copy of the Duke Pearson recording "Make It Good" from his album *The Right Touch*. Trumpeter Freddie Hubbard's solo begins at approximately 3:25 in the track. Learn it by ear and then play along, reading the rhythms as provided here. Which stickings work best? What are you learning about phrasing? Do this sort of thing enough, and I promise that you'll never be at a loss as to what to play when you have occasion to solo. By the way, that's Grady Tate playing the drums on this recording. The entire album is great.

Now let's play some time and swing with this play-along track!

3

Fast and Slow Tempos

Scene: A drum clinic.

"Any questions?"

Uncomfortable silence follows, with some mild squirming by the audience and clinician. Finally, a hand goes up. The young drummer in the fifth row asks, "How do you play fast tempos?"

The clinician sighs to himself and wonders, "Why doesn't anyone ever ask how to play a *slow* tempo?"

Perhaps it's natural for youth to be preoccupied with speed—be it racing cars, "Wipeout," or perhaps even "Cherokee." And, fair enough, it's necessary to be able to handle those fast tempos with, hopefully, some grace and aplomb. But let's not forget the challenge in playing slow.

The best advice I can give for playing either fast or slow is to play *relaxed*. In the case of the fast tempos, playing relaxed is the only way to go, because tightening up your muscles will only constrict your flow and movement. For the slow (and ultra-slow) tempos, relaxation is equally important, from the physical point of view as well as from the psyche's (or musical) point of view. You must trust that the notes you are playing are correct, and that the space in between each note gets its full duration. In other words, the "silence" is as important as any note that you might play.

Play the following ride cymbal pattern. Be sure to phrase the triplet as a true triplet.

BPM = 32–60

4

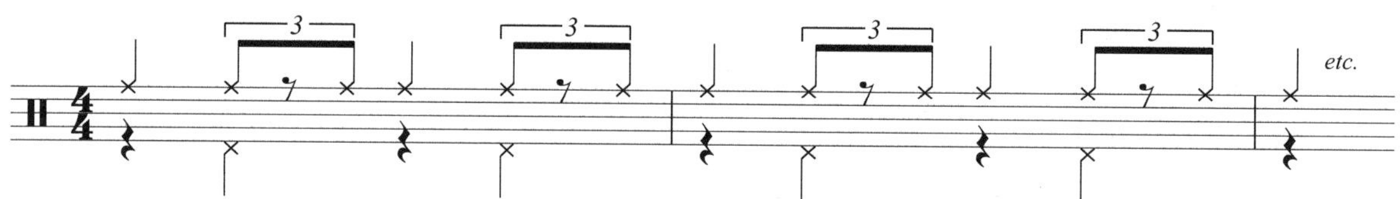

When you play such a slow tempo, it is important to concentrate. Consistency counts for a lot. I think of the bass player's fingers plucking the next note on the string when I play something like a real slow blues. You may want to think of it as a walk in the country—enjoy the scenery! It's not necessary, or desirable, to fill up all of those spaces in between the notes. Play relaxed and with conviction. It will sound good.

Compare the previous triplet phrase to the following dotted eighth/sixteenth-note phrase and the double-dotted eighth/thirty-second-note phrase.

5

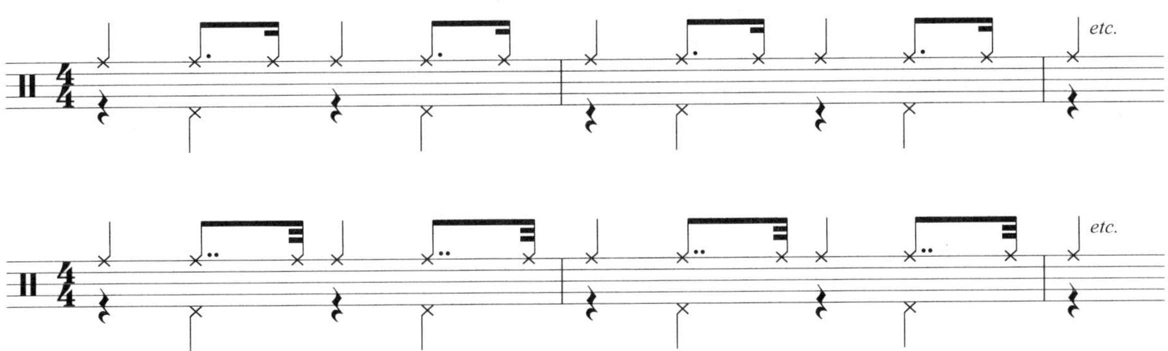

They certainly sound different from the triplet phrase. And they imply something different, too: double-time...

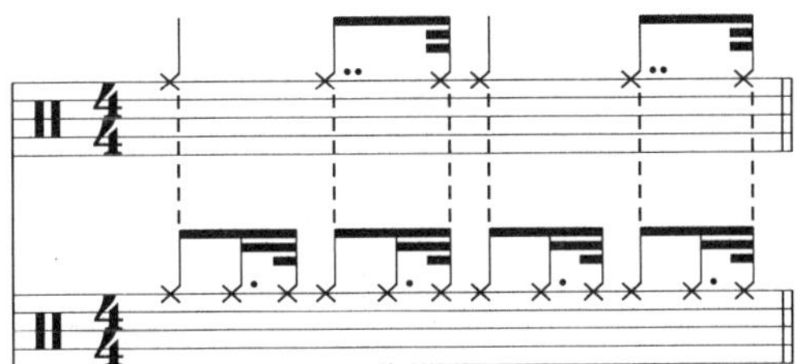

Be aware of the difference! When I was young, my father told me, “Say what you mean and mean what you say.” So if you’re playing a slow tempo and don’t mean to imply a double-time feel in the middle of a tune, then don’t do it!

Now, practice, play some music, and play time on this slow blues play-along track:

6

Here’s how I played over the previous track:

7

Speeding things up, the faster the tempo gets, the straighter the swung eighth note will get. There is no metronomic line of demarcation for this. You may wish to play the ride cymbal in an "eighth-notey" fashion at a moderate tempo. I occasionally like to swing the eighth notes well up into the tempo arena. It's up to you. However, beyond a certain point, the tempo will be too fast to play the ride cymbal pattern any other way than this (listen to Track 48, "November," on the accompanying audio files):

8

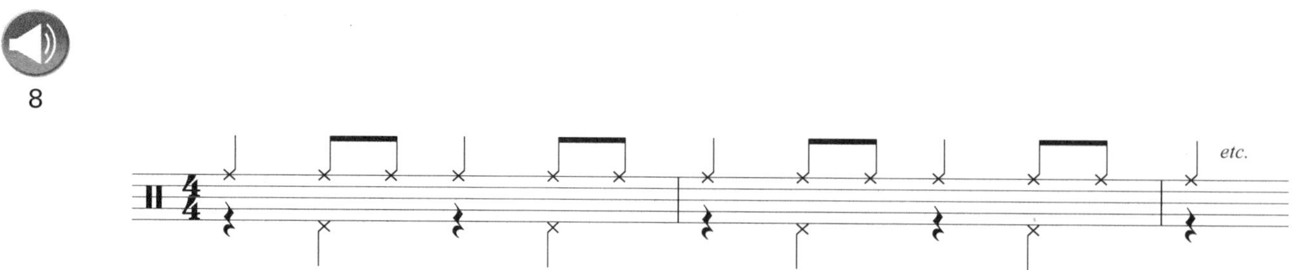

Find the tempo (metronome marking or BPM) where you can most comfortably play a fast ride-cymbal beat. Make note of it. Practice uptempo timekeeping every day, starting with just the ride cymbal and the hi-hat, and increase the tempo a little bit each day. Your ability and endurance should grow. Work on this carefully and slowly! Watch for bad habits, i.e., fingers awkwardly sticking out, unbecoming facial expressions, "rigor mortis" in the right arm, etc.

Keep it simple! Remember: There's not as much room in the fast tempo for all of the time-marking ("doggie-paddling") fill-ins on the snare drum. Think lean, clean, and light on your feet. Make it dance. And, since your consistency has no doubt improved because of your practice of basic time-keeping, now's the time for you to break up the ride-cymbal pattern. A little change-up here and there can relieve your muscles from their constant chore. (It can also serve to open up the texture from the drums.)

Whether you are playing slow or fast, keep your movements efficient, and don't engage in too much "air-drumming" (bringing your sticks way up in the air between strokes). You won't have enough time to do that in the fast tempos, and during the slow tempos, that habit will hamper your consistency.

Use a metronome for practice (preferably one with a headphone output or a drum machine), and keep track of your progress, both up and down the tempo spectrum.

One final word: When you practice, be sure to practice at different tempos, not just that medium tempo that you love so much. Bandleaders or conductors are liable to count off any tune at any tempo, and you'd better be able to make it feel reasonably good. Even if you're working with the same people night after night, you'd be surprised at the effect a good meal or too much coffee can have on a count-off.

My composition, "Autumn Rose," has enjoyed three live performances on CDs that were recorded in 1999 (*Live at Rocco*), 2009 (*The Interlochen Concert*), and 2014 (*Trio M/E/D*), in California, Michigan, and Italy, respectively. Audio Track 9 has the intro from each recording. Sometimes, a piece of music has its own tempo, no matter the time zone or setting. I'll admit to being impressed by these tempo similarities! (Note: The clicking sound is a cross-stick on the snare drum; no metronomes or click tracks were used for these performances.)

9

Phrases and Barlines

There is something about defining one's territory that is as comforting as it must be primitive. We see dogs do it all the time. Drummers do it too—not by periodically visiting the corners of our property, of course, but by establishing the "property lines" of musical phrases. As with all manners and forms of establishing territorial rights, some ways are more sophisticated than others.

I began my career in big bands, and in that situation there is a lot of structure. You're basically playing to serve the chart, and everything is fairly apparent in terms of the beginnings and ends of phrases.

One day at a rehearsal with the Stan Kenton band, I was hitting every accent and cutting every figure (something I think drummers sometimes do just to prove that they can actually read!). Afterwards one of the writers (Gene Roland) came up to me and said, "I've got fifteen guys hitting these figures. I don't need you to do it too." So I started thinking about ways that I could not be so obvious about everything.

I discovered that orchestration on the drumkit could make a big difference. Most drummers tend to end phrases by playing something on the snare drum and then hitting a cymbal and bass drum. BAM—there it is, right in your face. But you can often play the stronger part of the beat on the weaker part of the kit. You can hit the snare instead of the bass drum, and a lot of times I like to crash a small cymbal without a bass drum underneath. Texturally, it's wide open. It's like putting a lovely question mark at the end of a phrase; that leads you to the next phrase, instead of just ending every phrase with an exclamation point.

When I started playing with smaller groups, I was able to apply some other phrasing ideas. I was getting more and more experience playing music that wasn't so obviously boxed. I really sensed that I couldn't "gift-wrap" my phrases, ending them with the pat devices that would get me from one phrase to the next. For a more fluid kind of playing, there are no set licks.

Consider the following examples, typical of the younger or less-experienced player:

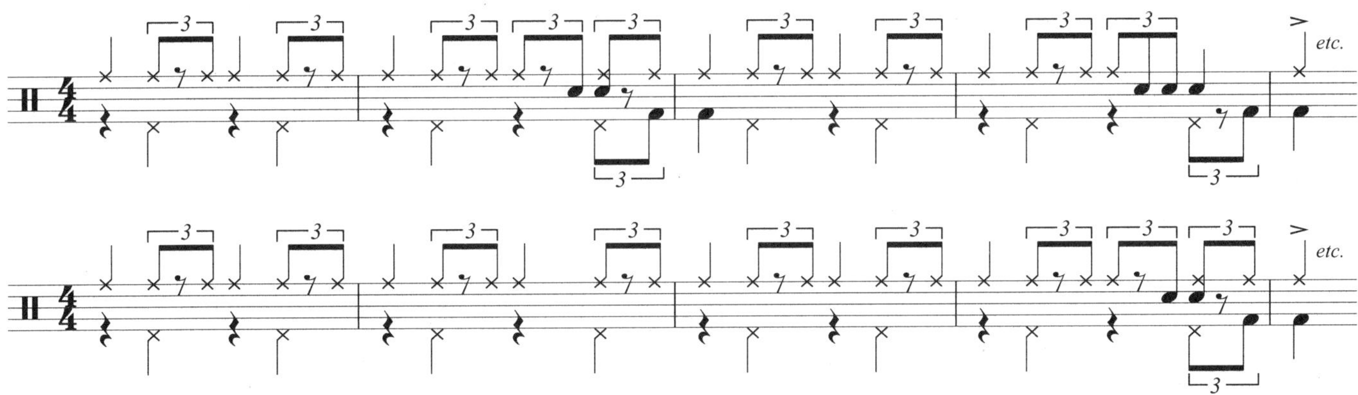

What's going on in the drummer's mind here? Well, based on personal experience, I'd have to guess that the drummer is delineating these phrases every two or four bars because that represents security. Landing the bass drum on good, old *terra firma* feels comfortable and safe. Why? Because the drummer doesn't have enough experience (or confidence) in basic timekeeping. If things feel a bit shaky in the music, a solid downbeat on the bass drum should cure that, right? These repetitive phrase markers are usually played over and over again without the drummer realizing it.

Once you develop your strengths on the ride cymbal, not only will you gain ability and confidence, but you will also start to internalize the time. I don't need to always keep the time going "ding, ding, ding" on the ride cymbal. I did for a long time. When you first start out, it's really important to develop that concept and ability of keeping time on the cymbal. But eventually, you can internalize that feeling—that knowledge—so that you can then not play it and the time will still be there. Then, you can start experimenting with different phrasings.

One approach is to play the swung eighth-note subdivisions in different parts of the bar. But always keep a strong focus. Imagine the ride cymbal is the string on an acoustic bass and your stick is a finger plucking it. It's easy to just let a stick bounce over a cymbal, but a bass player has to make a very specific motion for each note, and I think that is a good way to approach playing the ride cymbal.

When you are comfortable doing that, you can get away from the steady quarter note and not state every beat. Maybe play the "and" of beat 4 and let it ring into the next beat, then pick it up again. Always keep the forward motion; when you start playing again, come in at exactly the right time.

Perhaps you have heard the expressions "inferred time" or "implied time." My computer's *American Heritage Dictionary* supplies the following definitions:

in•fer

1. To conclude from evidence or premises.
2. To reason from circumstance; surmise.
3. To lead to as a consequence or conclusion.
4. **To hint; imply.**

im•ply

1. To involve by logical necessity; entail.
2. **To express or indicate indirectly.**
3. *Obsolete*. To entangle.

Let's go with the definitions in **bold** print (though I also like definitions 1 and 2 for "infer"). In music, particularly jazz, these terms would indicate the use of less-than-obvious timekeeping devices. In other words, it is not necessary to play "ding, ding-a ding" all of the time, or in any given tune.

I did "The Music of Miles" with Gil Evans a number of times at the Hollywood Bowl, and Jimmy Cobb played some of the *Porgy and Bess* stuff—quarter notes on the ride with that fat cross-stick on beat 4. It blows your mind because it swings so much. About three years later, we played it at Disney Hall, but Jimmy Cobb wasn't on that concert. One of the *Porgy and Bess* things is "It Ain't Necessarily So," and Terence Blanchard was *dealing*—he's *playing*. It would have been very tempting to start tangling with that because it's so cool, but I only played quarter notes on the cymbal with a cross-stick on the snare. It was a long improvisation; Terence was soaring. We finished the tune, the audience went nuts, and what did Terence do? He walked back to me and pulled my hand up like I'm a champion boxer. I was just doing what Jimmy Cobb did, but it worked so great—that intuitive, magical brilliance of Jimmy Cobb.

I've worked a lot with Seth MacFarlane, who everybody knows from *Family Guy*, but he's a great singer and puts on a good show. He always talks about the great arrangers and refers to the time when music was more than three Swedish guys dicking around on a laptop. I did a record with Seth, *Music Is Better Than Words*, and we were recording direct to analog tape, so we either got a good take or we did it again. The first take was pretty much for running the tunes down, so I just played quarter notes on the ride cymbal, hi-hat on beats 2 and 4, and I kept a pencil in my left hand so I could mark certain brass figures on the part. We listened back, and I noticed the chart was swinging like crazy. So we did the next take, I had all the rhythms marked, and I was doing my perfect Alvin Stoller imitation with a bit of Shelly Manne, with all the setups and little fills. We finished the take and everyone was like, "That's it—a perfect take!" But when we were listening back, I turned to the bass player, Chuck Berghofer, and I said, "This doesn't swing as much as that first run-through," and he said, "Yeah, you're right." So I went up to Seth and the arranger/producer, Joel McNeely, and I said, "Hey guys, can we do one more?" Seth was having fun singing with a big band, so he said, "Sure!" Joel said, "OK, but why?" I said, "I think we can get it to swing more." The trumpet players were not happy about having to do it again, but we did it, and with the exception of a couple of spots here and there, I just played quarter notes on the ride and hi-hat on beats 2 and 4. No cross-stick, no setups, and it was that idea of not providing all the information, which invites the listener in and it becomes a participatory experience, as opposed to playing everything—which, to me, is not very interesting. The final result swung like crazy.

A recurring theme in most of my discussions concerning drumming is the importance of being able to play a simple beat well. I literally practice what I preach as much as possible! But, of course, drumming possibilities abound—the sky's the limit.

Creative timekeeping is not restricted to jazz music, of course. Funk, rock, fusion, and all manner of world musics combined with "Western" sensibilities or instrumentation have benefited from someone's creative urge to express the beat, or the song, in a slightly different way.

Don't Fence Me In

Music is linear. Interrupting the time with fills every few bars seriously lessens the flow of the music. I suggest that you record your playing as much as possible and give it a listen. If you hear yourself constantly setting things up for the next phrase, then you may not only be overdoing it, you may also be compensating for bad timekeeping by constantly re-establishing the beat's territory.

Don't box everything into four- or eight-bar phrases. You want to get away from those predictable blocks of timekeeping. I always play on the form of the tune, but within that, I might play a nine-bar phrase. That's part of "going over" the barline. It's like wearing baggy shorts and a T-shirt instead of a suit and tie.

Consider this example of a more open means of accenting and acknowledging the passage of a few bars' time:

10

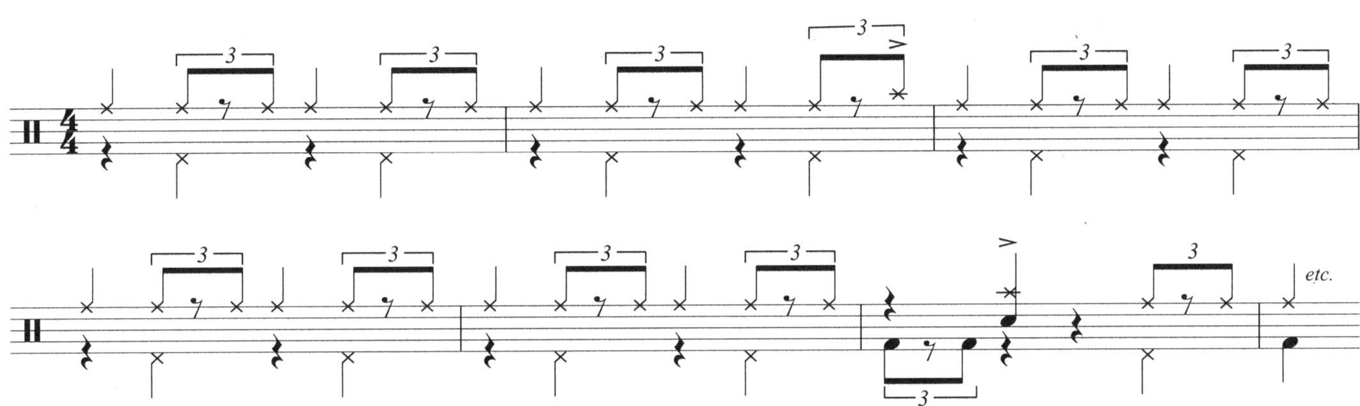

I think that breathes a little better. Remember that "creative" does not necessarily equal "busy." A few well-placed notes make a lot more music than a whole bunch of notes squeezed into a short amount of time.

Here are some ways of delineating the end of one bar (or phrase) and the beginning of the next:

11

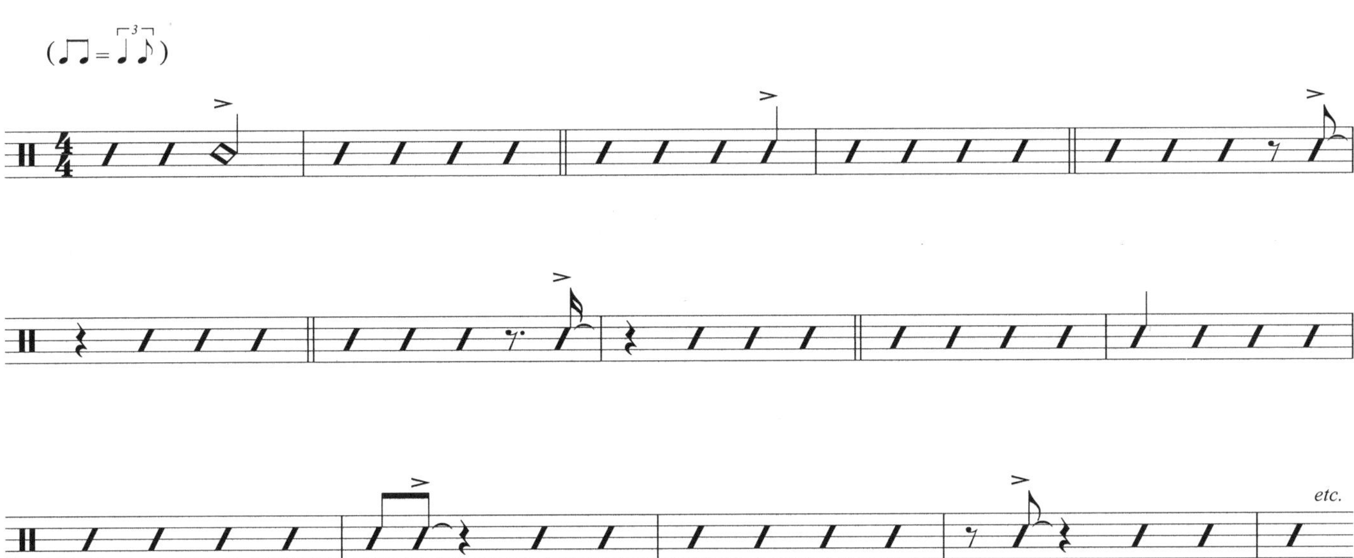

You can also let your fill go over the barline and extend past the downbeat, as in these next two examples.

12

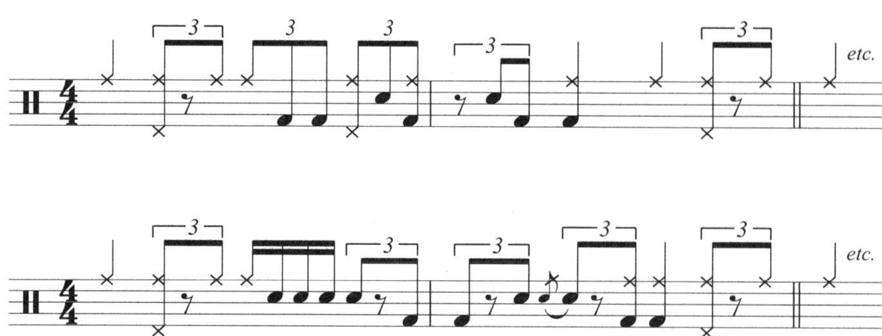

The interesting thing about these destination points is this: Are these meant to delineate the end of a phrase or the beginning of a phrase? And, in the spirit of the great jazz drumming pioneer Kenny Clarke, do these simple rhythms invite us to comment after the fact (after the phrase, or playing over the barline)? I like a good downbeat as much as the next musician. It was Shelly Manne, after all, who reminded me that, "You can't have a 2 and 4 without a 1 and 3."

The downbeat of a song may be approached creatively as well. There are more ways to begin a jazz tune than by playing:

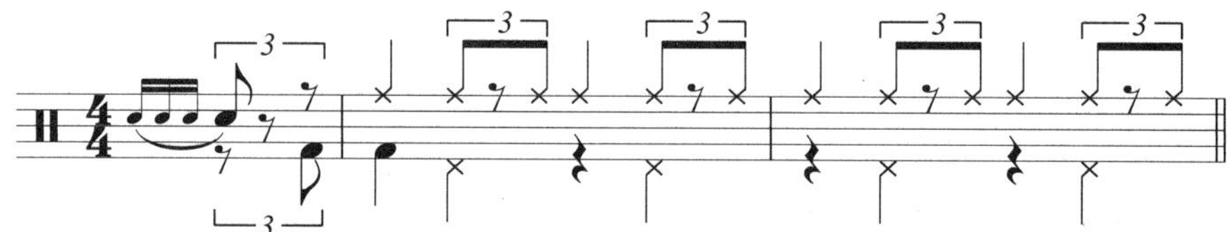

Consider the following suggestions. On the first beat of a tune, play just:

A. The bass drum and cymbal (crash or ride).
B. The bass drum.
C. The cymbal (ride or crash).
D. The snare drum (with the cymbal).
E. The snare drum or tom-tom without a cymbal.
F. The hi-hat (closed or open), with or without the bass drum.

Or, try no drums at all!

Unless the arrangement or composer (or band members, bandleader, etc.) asks otherwise, you can dare to play little or nothing at all. Whatever you do play, do it with conviction and open ears.

On one occasion when I was recording with a piano trio, for the beginning of the tune, I thought some light-textured drumming was called for. So I played time on just the ride cymbal (no hi-hat on beats 2 and 4 to start with). The ride cymbal was a Zildjian Flat Ride, with lots of "air" in the sound.

After we played the introduction a couple of times, I realized that enough rhythmic activity was already going on with the bass and piano. I felt that I could afford (indeed, the music was begging texturally for me) to play even less. I wound up playing just a single note on the Flat Ride every one or two bars for the first sixteen bars. Then, slowly, I added more notes, more rhythms, on more and more of the kit, until I was playing the tune in a straight-ahead fashion. Nobody told me to do it that way; it just felt most comfortable and seemed to work best for the music.

And that is why we play what we play!

Drummers do whatever they have to do to make themselves feel physically comfortable with the beat of the music. Make sure that what you do is appropriate and musical. As my father once told me, "Do what you want to do, but know why you're doing it."

Ensemble Playing

"You can take the drummer out of the big band, but you can't take the big band out of the drummer."

I'm not sure if the above sentiment is true, or even if it is, if that's such a bad thing. In recent years, small-group playing has become my favorite medium for making music with more than one person. But professionally, I did start out as a big band drummer. And I think that if you listen enough to any kind of music, you can capture its spirit and feeling, or its essence. No matter what your preference may be, some experience in large ensemble playing can be beneficial.

I'd like to address an important stylistic consideration: the "cutting" or "catching" of figures.

Consider the following rhythmic figure:

That's pretty common in jazz music arrangements. In drumset notation, the standard practice is: For any rhythm written within the staff, the drummer is expected (or encouraged) to play it, while rhythms written above the staff are for the benefit of the drummer's knowledge (i.e., all or part of the band will be playing that figure), and it is left to the drummer's discretion whether to "cut" it or not.

Here are some examples of fills and set-ups for that rhythm. (On the audio track, each example is preceded by one measure of time.)

13

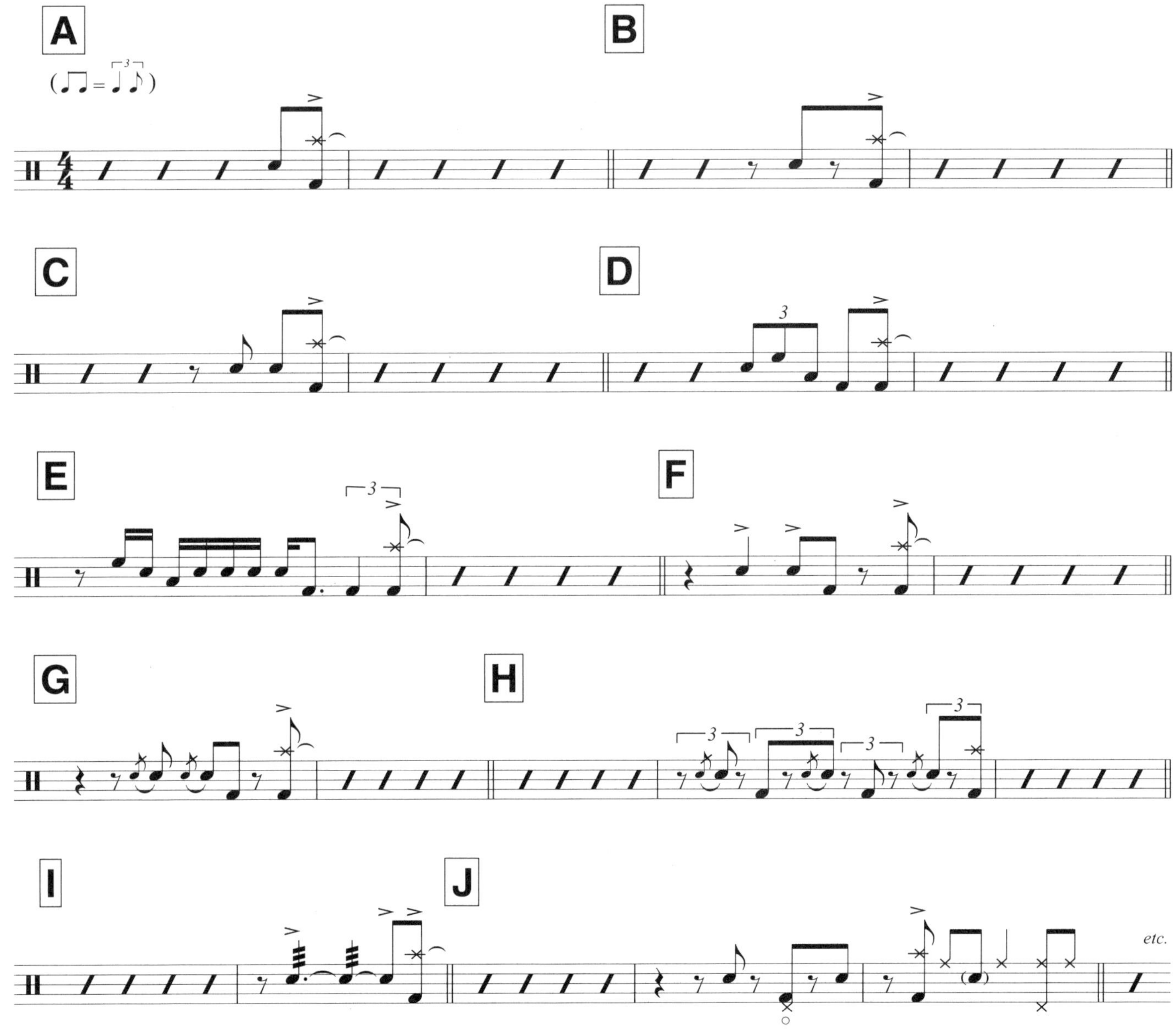

A

B

C

D

E

F

G

H

I

J

etc.

And so on. You can go from simple to complex, and from not too many notes to a whole lot of rhythmic activity. But here are some things to consider:

1. If, in a big band context, there are five, ten, or fifteen horns playing a figure, that may be enough punctuation by itself, without the drummer having to play the figure as well. Too much catching of all the horn figures, and the jazz band can start to sound like a circus or show band.

   One really hip approach, perhaps best exemplified by the drumming genius of Mel Lewis, is to play the "holes" or "spaces" in the arrangement, i.e., play an accent or figure of your own creation between some of the band's tutti statements.

2. Orchestration on the drumkit becomes really important here. Consider the different sound possibilities: playing the bass drum/crash cymbal together; the snare drum/crash cymbal together; a rack or floor tom/crash cymbal together; just the bass drum by itself; the snare drum by itself; a tom-tom; or the crash cymbal by itself (or whatever sound you may have lurking behind that electronic drum pad/trigger). One thing that I can tell you is that a rhythm on the "and" of beat 4 tends to lead somewhere, and your playing should have the effect of stepping off of the curb with one foot and continuing your trek with the other—not jumping off of the curb and landing with both feet... in the mud!

3. Jazz music's essence is improvisation. The music is like a dialogue. Sometimes, it sounds good to play a rhythm before or after the figure and not actually catch the figure that the rest of the group is playing—kind of like you're making a suggestion (or an afterthought) to the band.

4. If you're going to be playing a chart in a big band, and that chart has been recorded, listen to the recording and notice how that drummer interpreted the part. There are no rules when it comes to drumset reading. In fact, I think that the most important element for a drummer to have in reading a drum chart is a good pair of ears. Listen to what the rest of the band is doing. And if you've got the opportunity to study someone else's interpretation, then take advantage of it. Interpretation is what drumset reading is all about.

5. Don't always use the same fill-ins or set-ups for a particular figure. Be creative. (Just don't play "stump the band" too often; remember that a fill should take the music from where it was to where it's going, and the downbeat should not be too big of a mystery—for yourself or anyone else in the group.)

6. Don't approach the same rhythms in a small group the way you might in a big band. And watch the tendency to catch too many of the figures, whether written or not, that the band may be playing.

   Of course, the same rules for musicality apply here as anywhere else: Keep good time, use discretion, and play with dynamics. ("Whadd'ya mean, use more dynamics? I'm playing as loud as I can!")

Regarding points 1, 3, and 4, please refer to the audio tracks that accompany this book: Track 41 ("Know Where You Are") and Track 46 ("Elvin's Mambo") are both good demonstrations of various drumming approaches to supporting ensemble figures, as well as playing "around" them. Chapter 17 offers specific commentary about these examples.

CHAPTER 4

ORCHESTRATION ON THE DRUMSET

> *"When someone who doesn't know how to swim is thrown into the water, instinct tells his body what movements will save him. The artist, too, is driven by a kind of instinct..."*
>
> —Andrei Tarkovsky

There are limitless possibilities in terms of the ways you can orchestrate something you're playing on the kit. The most basic example would be a snare drum backbeat in a pop context. Do you play it in the center of the drumhead or a little off center, or do you play a rimshot or a cross-stick? Each of these four variations will affect the way the beat sounds and lays within a piece of music. You could then decide to move that backbeat from the snare to one of the tom-toms or perhaps play it on the bass drum.

It's always good to remain open when you're playing any piece of music, particularly something that comes your way the first time. For example, drummers learn a bossa nova beat, and that's what they play whenever a bossa nova tune is called. But instead of, say, always playing the hi-hat with the right-hand stick, you could hold a brush in your right hand and tap the surface of the head with it or swish the brush back and forth to simulate a shaker.

If I'm playing a bossa nova or samba, and the tempo is on the bright side but the dynamic is low because it's a trio or I'm working with a vocalist, I've found it very effective to play the rhythms on the hi-hat alone, and maybe just use the bass drum on the main pulses.

15

Bossa Nova

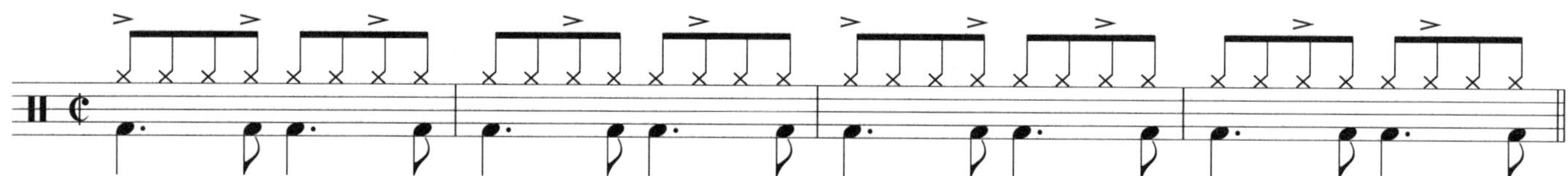

Samba

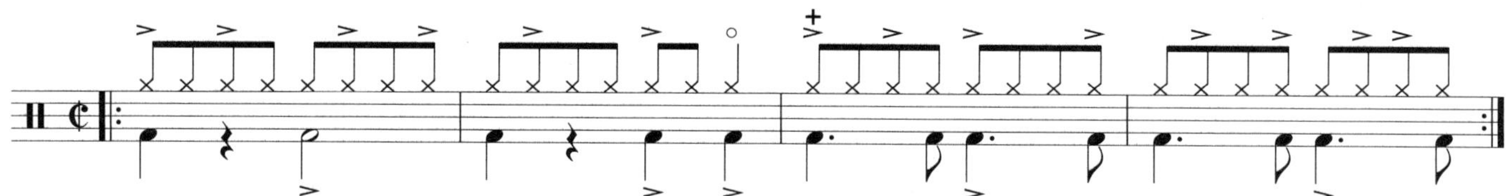

Adding the bass drum, I play the first note of the bar with a "dead" stroke (letting the beater rest against the head to muffle the stroke), and bouncing the beater off the head for an "open" stroke. This suggests or sounds like the Brazilian *surdo* drum (the second half of the bar is accented).

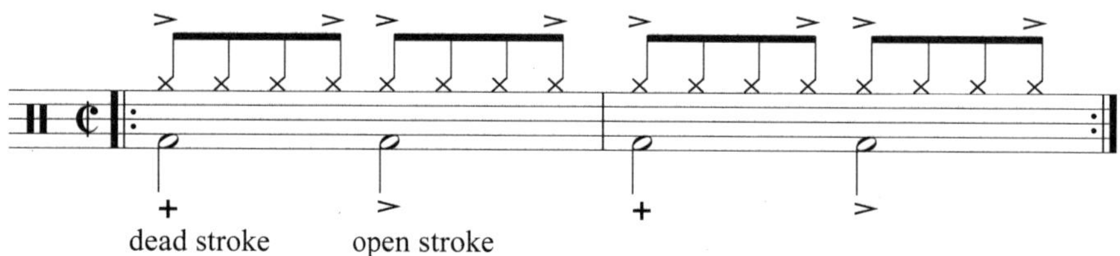

Do all of this while playing the inverted double-stroke sticking I've notated.

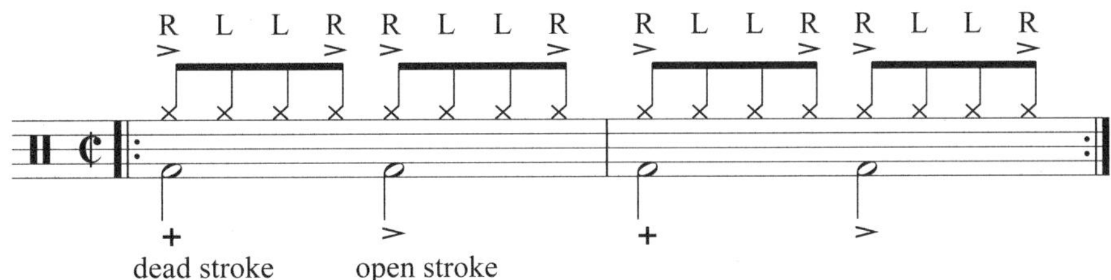

First: Play just the right hand and swing those notes like a shuffle.

Next: Play just the left hand, being very exact with the note placements.

Combine these two feels; this is the beginning of being able to play the Brazilian feel (OK, it's a cheat, but it works!).

Note: The right hand can be accented to your taste.

So I make a conscious choice to not orchestrate the beat as I was originally taught—left hand plays clave rhythm with cross-stick, right hand does eighth notes on the hi-hat, with the bass drum playing the typical drumset/samba rhythm.

I can capture the same rhythmic feeling, but I'm not having to walk on eggs by trying to play so lightly. I can comfortably keep the pulse going on the hi-hat alone, playing accents to imply a complete drumset beat, and that gives me dynamic and textural room to grow. It leaves my head clear; I'm not all tied up trying to play the original pattern I learned at a tempo that might not be so well suited for that particular beat. I can play the music in a very relaxed fashion, and that's the best thing for the music at that moment.

Another type of samba beat that I enjoy using is one that was inspired by something that Brazilian pianist Eliane Elias once sang to me. She said, "You Americans don't know how to sing samba; you all sound like TI-KA TI-KA TI-KA TI-KA." I smirked and said, "Well then, how should it sound?" She sang, "duh-goosh-ga, DO-goosh-ga, duh-goosh-ga, DO-goosh-ga." I imitate that with a pattern that combines drums with a surdo and *pandeiro* effect.

16

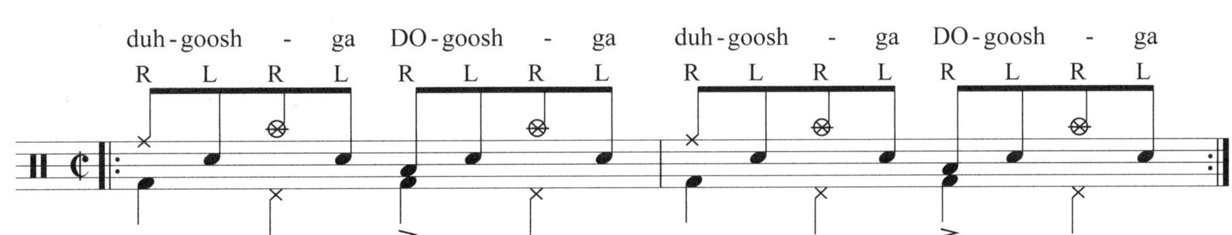

The next example has an almost *batucada* sound (samba percussion ensemble, basically) with the left hand playing on the hi-hat while it is opening and closing in order to do its own 2-and-4 thing; catching the hat in mid-air, as it were, creates a rhythmic element on its own. Like magic!

17

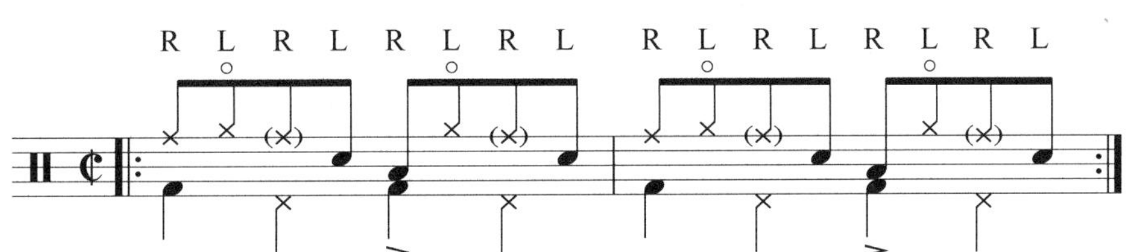

So orchestration is not just a matter of deciding where to put what. It's also a concept of looking creatively at the infinite choices of how to set a beat into motion and have it serve the music the best way. Going back to that bossa nova, the tempo and dynamics of the tune suggested that I do something on another part of the kit than what might have normally occurred to me.

A lot of times, in the middle of a jazz tune, I'll just start playing on the snare drum, almost like a New Orleans second-line kind of thing (but not exactly like that). Deciding whether to play the bass drum on all four beats in the bar in a jazz or swing tune is another example of an orchestration consideration.

The idea is not to be locked into any one mind set, or into a couple of muscle-sets, in terms of playing. Less-experienced drummers tend to rely on the same devices over and over.

Ultimately, a musician has to follow his or her musical instincts. The more listening you have done, the better informed those judgment calls will be. I will consciously call upon, say, a Mel Lewis orchestration or rhythmic option when I'm playing particular kinds of big band things, as opposed to if I'm doing a Basie or Buddy Rich chart—although I may integrate elements of all three of those styles into something.

The bottom line is that it has to be effective and sound good. When I worked with John Abercrombie, I noticed that if I played rhythms on my rack toms when he was soloing, it messed up the articulation for both of us because the tom-toms were in the same mid-range sonic register as his guitar. So when John was in a particular register of the guitar, I consciously would not use those drums. In other words, I would change my improvisational and rhythmic reactions to what he was doing based on the sonic considerations.

Playing the stand-up cocktail kit is terrific fun. I'm relying on a fresh rhythmic approach every time I step up to it. The hands aren't going to move the same way they're used to moving on the standard kit. So my choices become that much more specific when I'm playing. I'm a big advocate of putting people in situations where they can't rely on stuff they know and play out of muscle habit. Whenever I made ECM albums, that was constantly the challenge because producer Manfred Eicher would smell habits right away, and he might imply that I should play a particular part of a tune just on cymbals, for example.

My teacher, George Gaber at Indiana University, was always telling me to take only a hi-hat, bass drum, snare drum, and cymbal to a gig. I wanted to take everything, but he would say, "No, you'll be surprised what you come up with."

He was right. I think a lot of drum setups get distracting; it's hard to keep your focus. Every drummer should, on occasion, go out and play with as minimal a drumset as possible. It not only challenges your imagination, but it proves how resourceful and musical you can actually be. For me, it's an enjoyable challenge that makes it more interesting and fun. I feel better about my drumming when I make something happen on a smaller kit.

On the other hand, more sounds are, well... more sounds! Here are two video performances where I'm playing along with the Bob Mintzer Big Band (courtesy of the MINTZER big band app)—"Ellis Island," where I'm demonstrating multiple splash cymbals for the Zildjian company, and "Havin' Some Fun," in which I'm playing everything I could possibly want to play using just a ride cymbal and a pair of hats—and I'm enjoying myself both ways.

1: "Ellis Island"

2: "Havin' Some Fun"

A lot of drummers might be familiar with the Steve Gadd video where he plays on a cardboard box with brushes—and it sounds great! I have some recordings where Shelly Manne plays brushes on a small suitcase. It sounds really cool and you don't miss the rest of the kit. So if you can make something swing with a pair of brushes and a phone book, then you'll have that much more confidence when you sit behind a full kit. If you've ever had the opportunity to hear Jeff Hamilton play the brushes, you'll know what I mean.

Granted, it's cool to have a lot of things to hit. When I did a Steely Dan tour, the dynamic of the music called for having a few more cymbals than usual for crashes. It was nice to have four tom-toms instead of just a couple, and it was cool having the little sopranino snare drum for highlighting certain accents.

By the same token, sometimes you do a tour where you can't take your own kit, and it's a "drums du jour" situation where you use a different rented kit each gig. You can maybe carry a couple of cymbals, a snare drum, bass drum pedal, stick bag, and that's it. It's sometimes fun to play on different kits, and if it only has a couple of toms, then my drumming has to be, in a sense, that much better. A lot of jazz things I like to play with an 18-inch bass drum that's tuned high, but sometimes I have to play a large, dead bass drum, so I do it.

The sound of the instrument, and the sound of the instrument in the room, is going to determine what I'm going to play. But some drummers don't operate this way—Tony Williams didn't. Whatever the context, he played his drums the way he played his drums. And I respect that. But it's not my way, usually. Because I make my living making music in a variety of circumstances, I choose not to form a sort of icon of my playing personality, demanding that music meet me on my terms. I'm more than happy to meet a number of musical situations in each specific case's terms, while still maintaining my own sense of aesthetics or principles.

"Not a Word"

To illustrate some orchestration styles and options available to you for playing ballads and slow tempos, I will draw an example from a solo recording I made a few years ago, *Motion Poet* (on the Denon label). The song's name is "Not a Word." The full version appears on Track 43 in the audio files that accompany this book.

"Not a Word" starts, drum-wise, as any typical ballad might, with a slow, quarter-note pulse played with brushes and emphasized with a soft 18" K sizzle cymbal note, every so often. (By the way, try mounting your sizzle rivets like this: three rivets, spaced close together, on the lighter, or opposite, side of the cymbal. Louie Bellson had his rivets mounted that way, and I do it the same way now; there seems to be better control of, and sound from, the cymbal.) Otherwise, there is very little punctuation, or "cutting," of the band figures.

You should approach any ballad with an attitude of great patience. You can't seem to want to be in a hurry to finish the song. This requires great trust in the other musicians and, most importantly, in yourself. Know that the relative "little" that you're doing is quite enough. Laying the "pad" and keeping the time prepares the music for greater things to come.

For John Abercrombie's guitar solo, the arrangement (by Vince Mendoza) goes into a double-time feel, but with straight eighth notes. It is similar to a rhumba (at the session, we referred to this part as "the Pete Cha-Cha"). Again, patience and subtlety are begged for here, so using the brushes, I play a guiro-like pattern with the right hand, accenting (or lifting) the left-hand pulse on the "and" of beats 1 and 3, with the hi-hat on beats 2 and 4 (remember, this is double time), and the bass drum on the (slow meter) backbeat. (We've only included the drum part here for Track 18.)

18

The bass drum played on the backbeat is a great gift that we can thank, among others, Steve Gadd for, as well as Grady Tate, who played on Roberta Flack's recording of "Killing Me Softly." Anyway, as the song progresses, I pick up a stick and start to play (softly) beats 1 and 3 on the sizzle cymbal. The ride cymbal activity picks up as we go along until I get to eighth notes on the cymbal.

By now, the bass drum is being played on the downbeat of the bar, but I don't want to play backbeats on the snare drum. (Horrors! I've often heard drummers, particularly in high school big bands, resort to this on any ballad whenever the rest of the band starts to get loud.) On a ballad, the backbeat can be played on a deep-sounding tom, the bass drum, a crash cymbal (with no other punctuation and played with a sweeping motion on the edge of the cymbal), or as a cross-stick on the snare drum. Remember that by your orchestration on the drumset, you can respect the mood and emotion of the music—or you can totally foul it up.

If you're working with a singer, you'll certainly want to know, lyrically, what the song is about. Know the lyrics. Tell a story. This is good advice if you're playing just instrumental music as well. And, as always, strive to be musical!

CHAPTER 5

COMPOSING/IMPROVISING ON THE DRUMS

"Never did Mozart write for eternity, and it is for precisely this reason that much of what he wrote is for eternity."

—Albert Einstein

Drum books and many articles in drum magazines are full of examples of licks and patterns to play, beats and transcriptions to learn, and fills for almost any occasion, be it the big band or heavy-metal double-bass drum genre.

I've felt strongly, for a long time, that instead of seducing and encouraging the younger and learning drummer to practice, among other things, funk-rock beats in 7/4, odd-time sambas(!), or other marginally important aspects of the craft, young drummers should be encouraged to think, to play creatively, and to compose on the instrument. In other words, they need to play what they hear and imagine, not just play what their hands might know.

It is important for the creative musician to compose when he or she plays. By this, I mean that the player will exercise creative choices on the instrument—rhythmically, tonally, and texturally. The player will respond to the music in a musical way and not churn out something that just the "hands know"—but not the heart and mind. For example, a lick learned off of an album is something that was played by a particular drummer for a particular reason at the particular time that selection was performed and recorded. To regurgitate that lick time and again, in whatever context, is uncreative.

One compositional approach to playing involves the concept of "theme and variations." The "theme" can be thought of as the essential beat, or choice of rhythms and orchestration on the kit, that is used to state the song. The "variations" are the development of that original idea (theme).

It is essential to incorporate these musical expressions in such a way as to weave them into the fabric of the song. One way of approaching realization and performance in this regard is to seek what I call the "line" or "horizon" of a piece of music. What is its shape? Where is it going? What does it all mean? What does it all add up to in the end?

These are the same concerns a composer has with any piece of music. If you "compose" as you play, then you are approaching music in the most creative way possible.

Fills and, more distinctly, solos, are where a musician's lack of creative training can really show. Here is one system for developing your composing sense on the drums.

First, we want to establish some sort of ostinato upon which to build our improvisatory ventures. (The *Harvard Dictionary of Music* defines ostinato as, "A clearly defined phrase that is repeated persistently, usually in immediate succession, throughout a composition or a section.") A drum machine or computer sequencer (DAW, or digital audio workstation) is perfect for this. Program in a rhythm that is not too busy but will give you space, as well as a constant on which to work.

Below is a mambo beat that you can program into your drum machine:

Congas: S = slap; o = open tone; P = palm; FT = fingertips; M = mute
Timbales: + = dead stroke; o = open tone
Bongos: S = slap; o = open tone
Cowbell: o = open tone; + = muted tone

You could add something like this mambo to the above pattern:

Or, you can simply play along with the audio track provided here:

19

Audio track from the *Afro-Cuban Essentials* play-along app, available on the App Store, courtesy of Fuzzy Music, LLC.
Musicians: Otmaro Ruiz, piano; Rigoberto Lopez, bass; Aaron Serfaty, percussion.

Or, you can work with no machine or audio track at all. Create an ostinato pattern yourself. Here's one that I like to use—changing locales, a variation on the Brazilian *baião*:

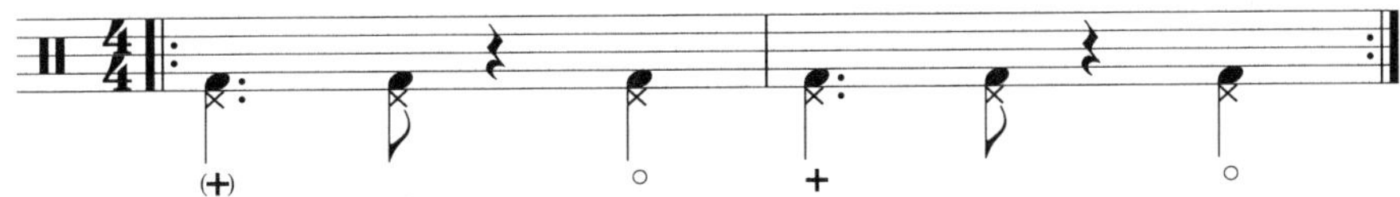

Whichever way we go with the ostinato, the next rule applies: DISCIPLINE YOURSELF. Start with a simple set of note choices to work with. By limiting your rhythmic and tonal choices, you can concentrate on the music you are actually making. Otherwise, the tendency is always to play "licks."

Improvise, starting on the small tom-tom, and then you can add another drum—say the snare drum. For now, no rolls! Play only combinations of quarter- and eighth-note rhythms (and rests), utilizing accents and dynamics. "Tell a story."

As the fixed-pitch instrument player has basically twelve tones to deal with, the rhythmic improviser has a relatively plain and simple palette, too. You've got whole notes, half notes, quarter notes, eighth notes, sixteenth notes, and dotted variations thereof. You've got triplets, rests, and infinite combinations of all of those. (Note: The audio example starts with the previous notated example and continues with the next example.)

By exploring the effectiveness of the simpler combinations, you can get a glimpse of what rhythmic creativity is all about. Don't just be fast and fancy. Use space, taste, and your ears—not just your feet and hands.

I hope that instead of feeling limited and constrained by this suggested regimen, you will start to feel liberated! The tools of improvisation and creativity are in your mind and heart, as well as in your hands.

Meanwhile, here's a delicious Art Blakey device for you to have fun with. Art plays this in duet with Philly Joe Jones on the tune "Wee Dot" from the epochal album *Gretsch Night at Birdland (Vol. 1)*. Blakey plays this, first on top of his own quarter-note bass drum pulse, and then atop an eighth-note triplet bass drum beat, while Philly Joe plays time.

Notice the double strokes bracketed by the number "2" in the notation. At first glance, rhythmically, these strokes may seem confusing—it's almost like the rhythms don't add up. However, when you listen to the solo, you'll hear that Blakey utilizes 5-stroke rolls unconventionally. While accuracy in transcribing exact rhythms is valuable and desirable, it's more important in this case that we understand the *larger outline* of what Blakey is doing here. Once we understand Blakey's placement of the roll in the context of the phrases, then we can apply it to our own playing. When playing these 5-stroke rolls, you should eventually "press" the double strokes (without too much pressure) to create more strokes and textures.

CHAPTER 6
ADVANCED CONCEPTS

> *"After silence, that which comes nearest to expressing the inexpressible is music."*
>
> —Aldous Huxley

Stickings: Their Impact on Rhythm Realization

Sound and Feel

Using different stickings changes the way rhythms speak on the instrument because we're not drum machines. Right and left strokes do sound different. For me, that's one of the great charms of wood-tip sticks—that element of change or chance. The tone of the sticks sound different. For example, Vic Firth Inc. computer-matches individual pairs of sticks, but once I throw them all in a stick bag, I don't worry about picking out a "matched" pair. Plus, cymbals sound different, and drums sound different. *Viva la difference*! That's why everyone isn't out there playing that same electronic kit.

Speaking of electronic drumkits, despite many technological advances, there is still a basic flaw in the approach most people take when utilizing these sound sources: how to articulate multiple strokes within a phrase or pattern. The problem is that "drumistic" stickings are not usually taken into account by the programmer; i.e., repetitive sounds have a machine-gun-like quality to them, and any illusion of an acoustic instrument being heard is pretty quickly destroyed. Left and right stickings are a crucial part of musical subtlety on the drums. (Since I have ventured into these waters by producing various sample libraries, I was quite intent on including left and right stickings for most every drum and hi-hat sound.)

Here's a nice example of the difference in sound a creative approach to stickings can make:

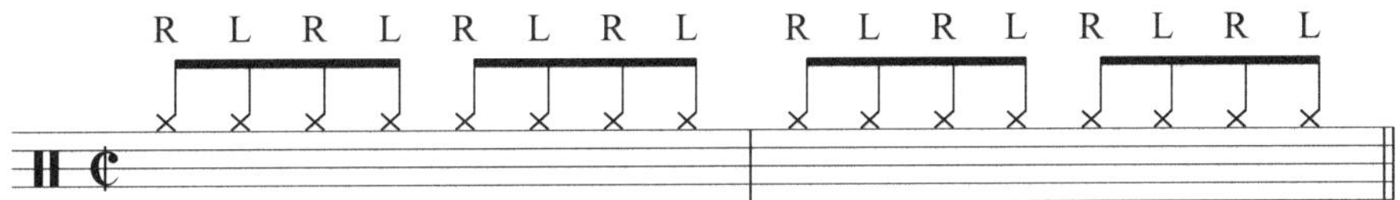

versus...

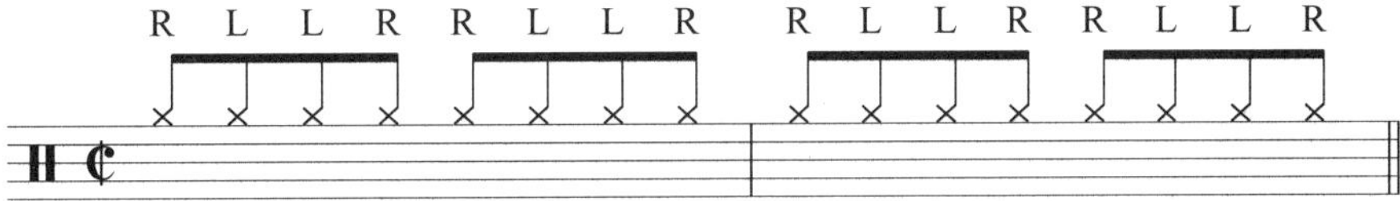

versus...

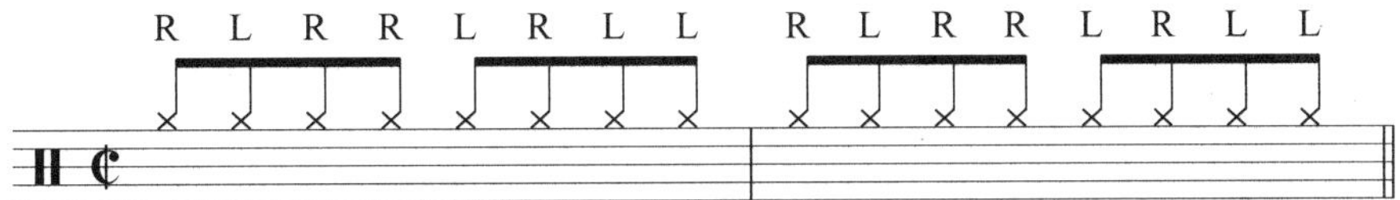

Eighth notes played on a closed hi-hat work well in a variety of situations (as accompaniment to a bass solo, or for use in an intro to a tune, or behind a soft/tutti section, etc.). Utilizing different stickings seems to almost automatically bring out a different feel—especially if the drummer is thinking of a particular type or style of subdivision! Try playing the previous examples with different stickings, and let the "wave" flow.

Logistics and Execution

When learning to play at different tempos, you have to reach the point at which you are able to, on the fly, plan your strokes ahead. It could be something as simple as, "I have to play a double stroke here so my right hand can get to that crash."

An exercise I sometimes practice, with and without a metronome, is playing eighth-note paradiddles on the snare drum, maintaining the hi-hat on beats 2 and 4, and then improvising on the bass drum.

Then, the bass drum assumes a rhythmic pattern, such as playing a baião (or "Charleston") beat, and I play paradiddles with accent variations.

Then, I combine those two things. If I've been away from the kit for a while, that exercise quickly gets me back in touch and in tune with the instrument.

21

R L R R L R L L R L R R L R L L R L R R L R L L R L R R L R L L *etc.*

Being open to different stickings can open up new drumming possibilities. For example, I used to always play triplets between my hands and foot R–L–F, R–L–F. Michael Brecker, who in addition to being a great saxophonist was also a pretty good drummer[2], pointed out to me that when Elvin Jones plays those triplets, a lot of times it's R–L–F, L–R–F, which has a whole different velocity to it.

22

2 Many outstanding instrumentalists are competent players of more than one instrument. One notable drummer who is not known primarily for his drumming skills is pianist Chick Corea (Jack DeJohnette is also a notable pianist!). Chick once relayed to me that he had wanted to "make it" as a drummer, but "unfortunately, the piano career started to take off"!

Something else I've started doing recently is to occasionally play the triplet pattern with the bass drum occurring in the middle of the triplet:

23

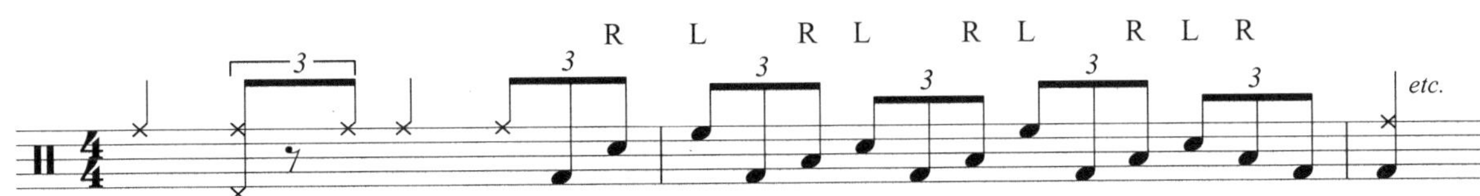

Something like that makes for a nice change of balance. Here are some more variations and exercises for you, based on everything we've been discussing.

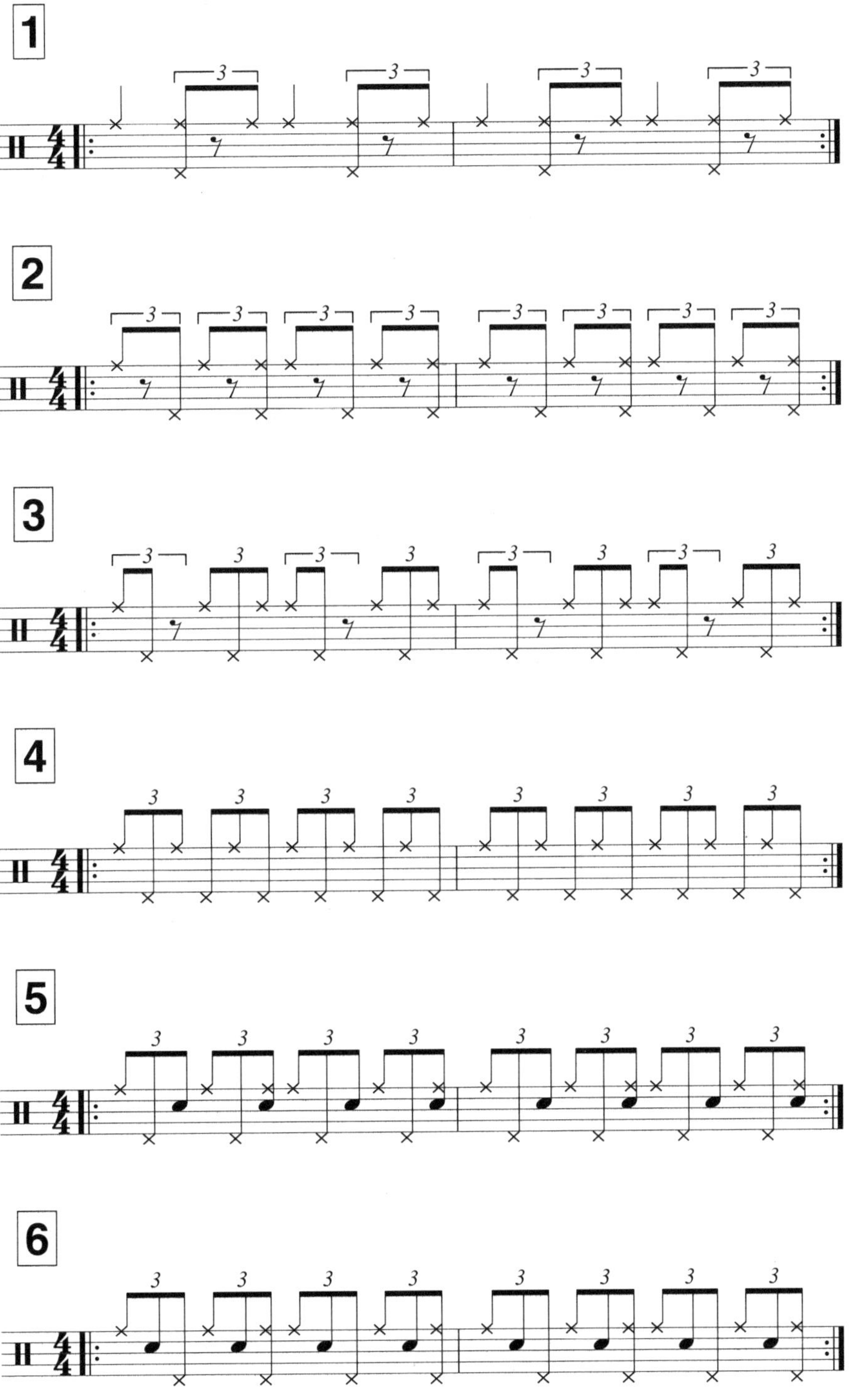

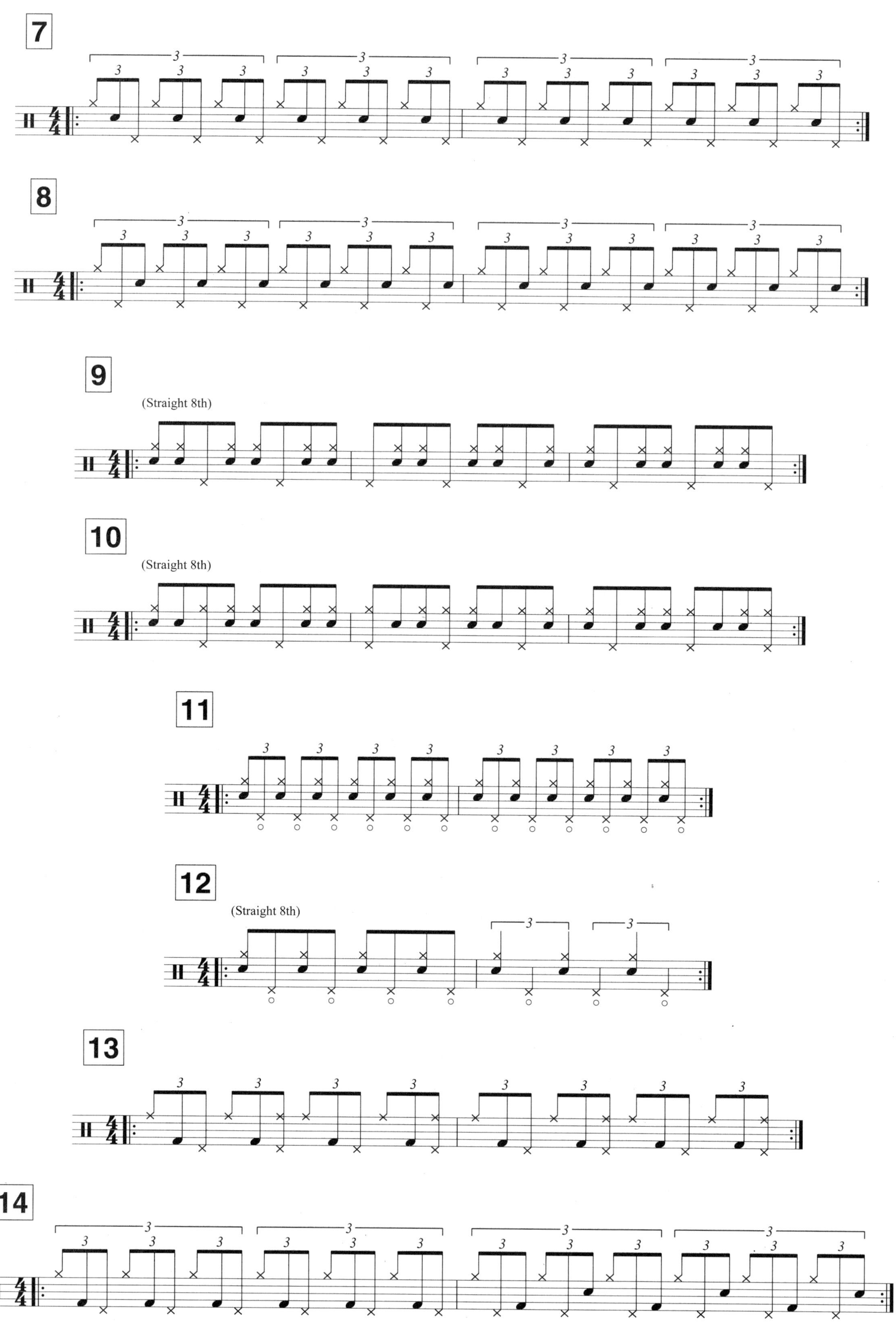
7
8
9
(Straight 8th)
10
(Straight 8th)
11
12
(Straight 8th)
13
14

15

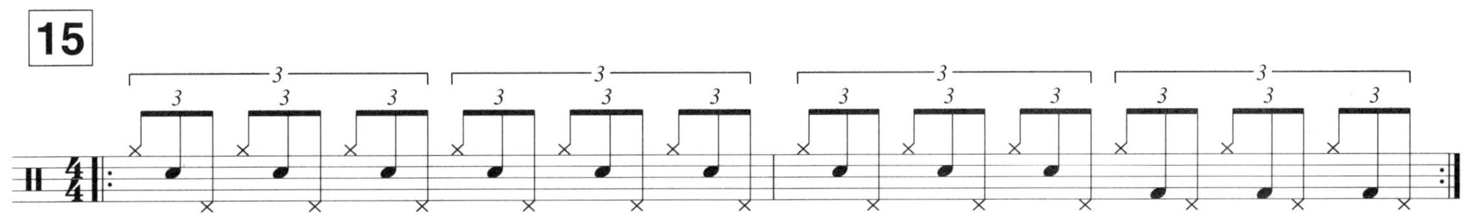

16

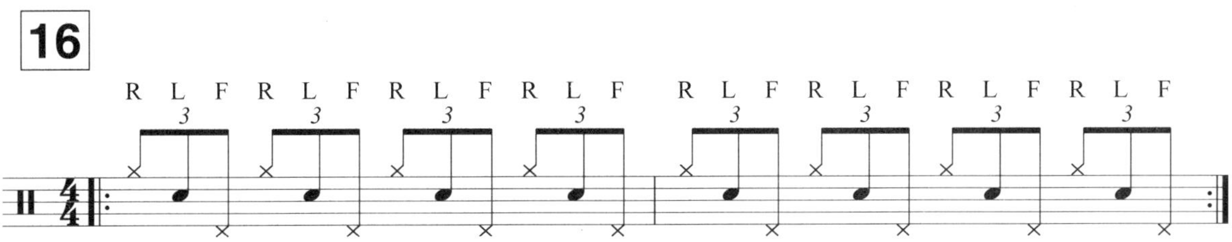

17

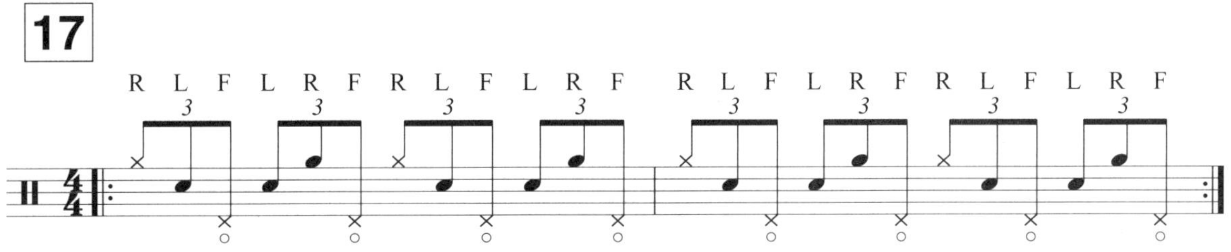

18

19

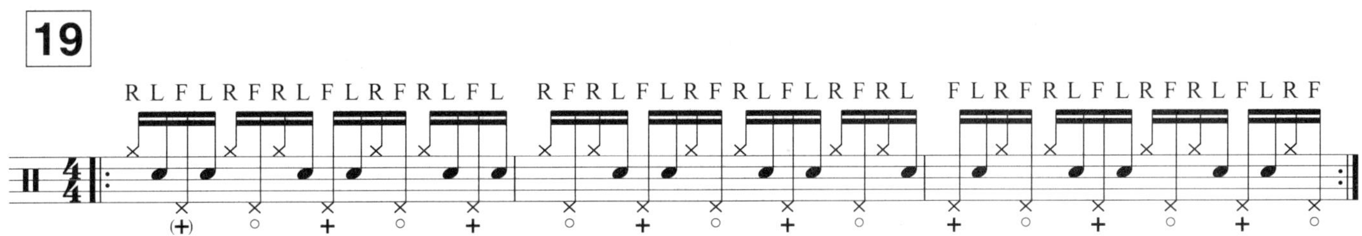

Don't just play technical exercises as written. You have to "run with them." Just sitting and playing countless variations of paradiddles or triplets doesn't encourage improvisation, doesn't encourage awareness of balance on the kit—it doesn't encourage awareness of a whole bunch of things you should be thinking of when you're playing. But you can play combinations of singles and doubles creatively at the kit and exercise all sorts of elements of your playing personality—texture, tone, dynamics, balance and, yes, chops. It's always important to concentrate and be aware of all of these factors when you play. And remember: Practicing IS playing.[3]

3 "I never practice, I always play." Quote by Wanda Landowska (famed harpsichordist and interpreter of the music of J.S. Bach).

Be aware, too, that one part of a rhythm pattern may be played on another part of the kit; for example, instead of always playing the third note of a triplet pattern on the bass drum (as part of "comping" on the kit), you can play it on the hi-hat instead.

24

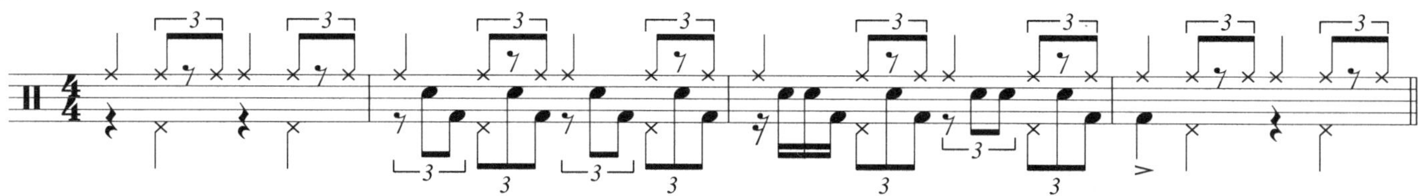

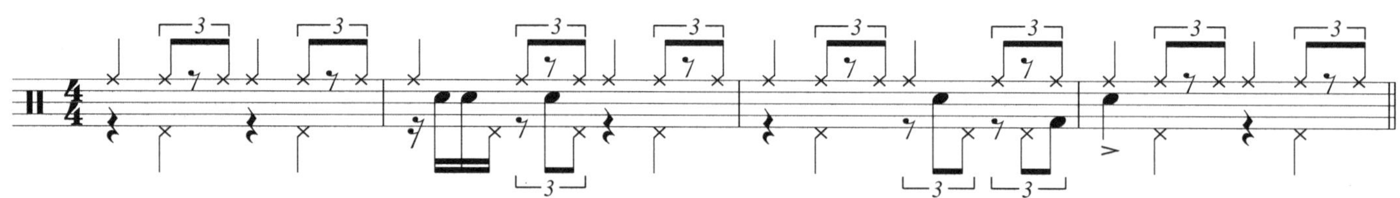

There are situations where you'll want to change the texture and weight of a drum statement while still maintaining the rhythmic essence. You'll know when to do this by *listening*.

Over the Barline

Once a drummer is confident that he or she can play a rhythm anywhere within the eighth-note, triplet, or sixteenth-note spectrum of subdivisions (like the exercises in my first book, *Drum Concepts and Techniques*, Hal Leonard) and not disturb the time flow, the interesting thing becomes to start playing in rhythmic groupings that aren't restricted to one bar but move over the bar. I hinted at that in my first book with the hemiola. Every three bars we come out on beat 1.

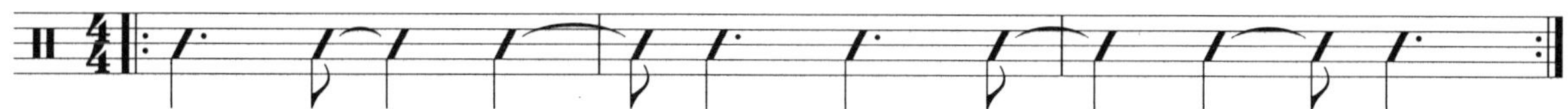

Now, let's extend it further. Instead of the space of three eighth notes, it could be the space of five eighth notes. You've got 4/4 in the cymbal with a five subdivision on the snare drum. (It could be a seven or whatever number.)

25

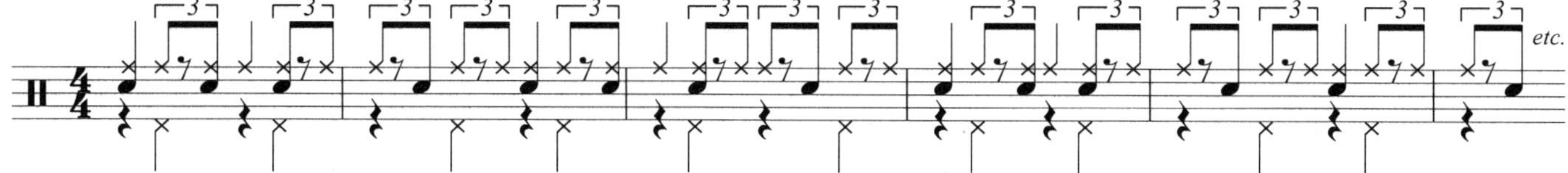

So you start creating architectural building blocks that, on one hand, are related to the jazz drumming vocabulary of Philly Joe Jones, Art Blakey, Jimmy Cobb, or Roy Haynes playing rhythms on the snare drum, but creating your own structure rather than using the bebop vocabulary. That's what you do in a lot of free music.

Then, you open up the ride cymbal (as in Rick Mattingly's book *Creative Timekeeping for the Contemporary Jazz Drummer,* Hal Leonard). Even though the internal reference is the standard jazz ride pattern:

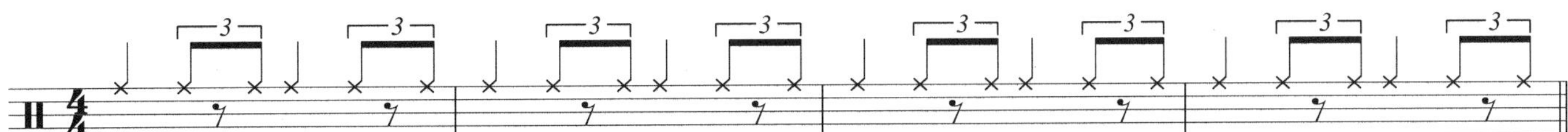

...you might be playing:

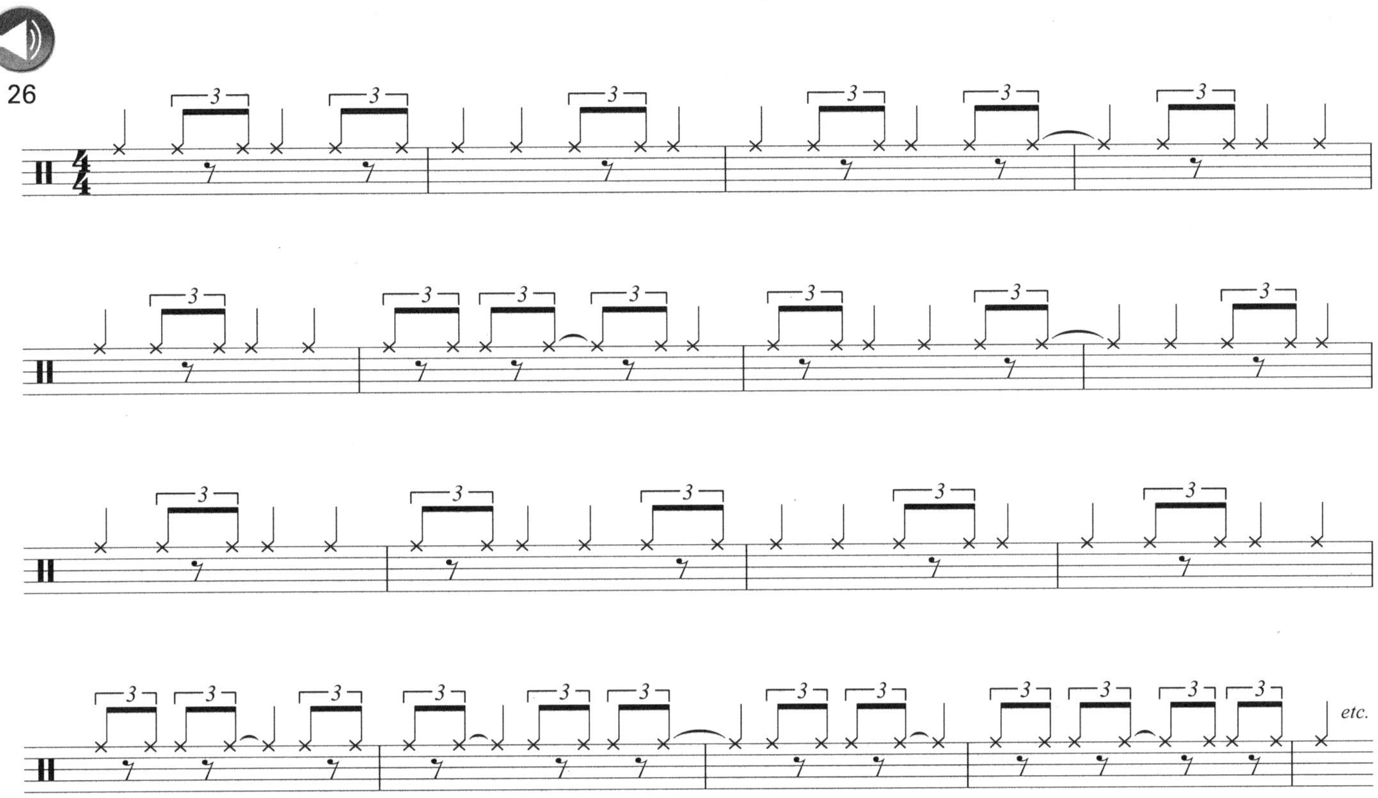

You first have to learn to play a basic beat really well because once that internalizes, then you can start doing these other things. And the reference point is always there, so it always swings and everything you play has meaning. But now, all of a sudden, you've taken what was pretty codified—the standard jazz ride pattern—and opened it up, expanding it. So you're not only drawing on traditional drumset vocabulary, but you're creating your own rhythmic structure for your interpretation of this tune that is being spontaneously created.

Even though the listener or other musicians hear:

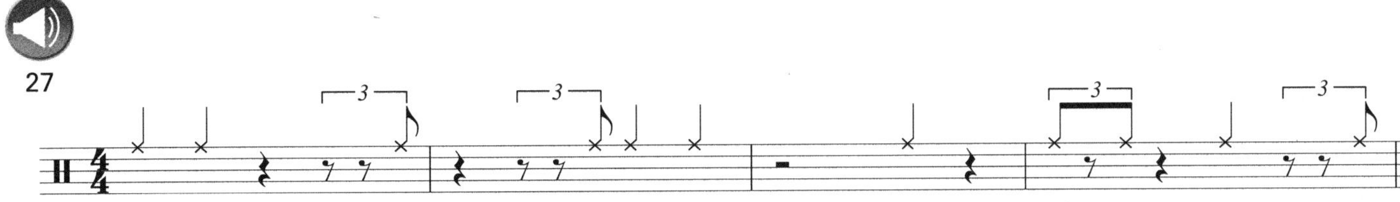

...which sounds almost random; but underneath, it's all:

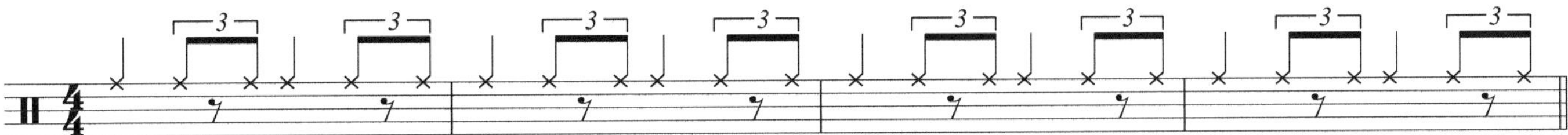

You imply the standard timekeeping pattern in such a way that, if your placement is tuned-in to that reference point, the music can swing just as hard.

Concerning playing over the barline, there are some very specific approaches that can ease a musician into becoming aware of the possibilities. When you think "free," it is still within a specific framework. You can extend one part of the phrase or compress it. Once a point of reference has been established, it's a very successful means of stretching and adding that element of creativity and surprise for the listener.

Another good exercise would be using relatively simple subdivisions with different rhythmic groupings, to get comfortable going over the barline. When you use triplets, fives, and sevens, it starts opening up a rich rhythmic palette.

Please listen to Track 48, "November," on the accompanying audio files; it's from an ECM recording I made with John Abercrombie and Marc Johnson. The piece is entirely improvised, and there's a refreshing lack of "one" throughout the playing. It floats, yet there are no concerns about barlines, or phrases being of a set number of measures. You'll be able to hear a wide variety of rhythmic groupings within the 4/4—NOT a 4/4 pulse.

Destination Points

Some drummers use very specific rhythms to get from one key accent to another. As complicated as some of it sounds, the patterns are very transcribable because the stickings and rhythms are so specific. But when you listen to drummers such as Jack DeJohnette or Elvin Jones, it's not always so easily transcribed. They'll simply move the sticks rapidly on whatever part of the instrument they're playing until it's time to hit the accent they want to hit.

In a sense, these multiple strokes function as rhythmic long tones on the drums. It's a very horn-like conception, which is a tremendous advance for the instrument. The phrasing is much more fluid, and it's really exciting because it becomes this "whirling dervish" kind of sound that just rolls out.[4]

So I stopped being aware of specific stickings and rhythms and started basically aiming for what I call "destination points" or accents. Sometimes just aiming for something and moving your hands works very well, as long as your destination point is on the money. As soon as you give up worrying about the specific stickings (which can be a very mechanical thing) in favor of a flurry of notes leading to an accurate destination, then you've reached another level of freedom in your playing.

Let's look at a very basic example of what I'm talking about. The following is a simple, effective way to get from the downbeat of one bar to the downbeat of the next.

Sometimes, though, we might want to create a feeling of momentum by starting out slowly and building the rhythmic intensity. Using the exact same number of notes, one could work out a very rhythmic way of achieving this effect, as in the following.

4 Keith Jarrett echoes this approach, as stated in the Jan./Feb. issue interview in *Piano & Keyboard* magazine: "Saxophone players in particular have influenced me. Not pianists. And if you think about Sonny Rollins, or Ornette (Coleman), (John) Coltrane, they're a voice. They have this freedom, and they're not percussive. They can play a river of notes and it doesn't matter what the number is. So when I'm playing piano, I don't want to hear the attack. I'm listening to this flow." Vladimir Horowitz said something similar: "I want to make the piano not a percussion instrument, but a singing instrument. The piano has to sing as much as it can." So, imagine the drums NOT as a percussive instrument! I don't know about you, but that revelation was a "light bulb" moment for me!

I have sometimes seen transcriptions of my own playing that resembled the previous example. (See the transcription for "Not an Exit" in Chapter 13.) I tip my hat to transcribers who are able to achieve such precision, but I have to say that—even though notation such as the above could be an absolutely accurate representation of what was played—in some cases it totally misses the point. When I wish to give the music some elasticity by starting slow and building to a rhythmic climax, I'm not always thinking about polyrhythms. I'm thinking about the musical effect, and my only concern is that I reach the downbeat of the next measure (or the "destination point") at the right time. What I am playing in such a situation could perhaps better be notated as follows.

To achieve such freedom, we must start with discipline. Our hands must be so fluent with different rhythmic groupings and stickings that when we play, we are not thinking about the mechanics of what we are doing—only the musical effect. The following exercise is a basic one for developing an awareness of different rhythmic groupings as well as for learning to land on a destination point with either hand. (The crash cymbal may be either on the right-hand or left-hand side of the kit.)

28

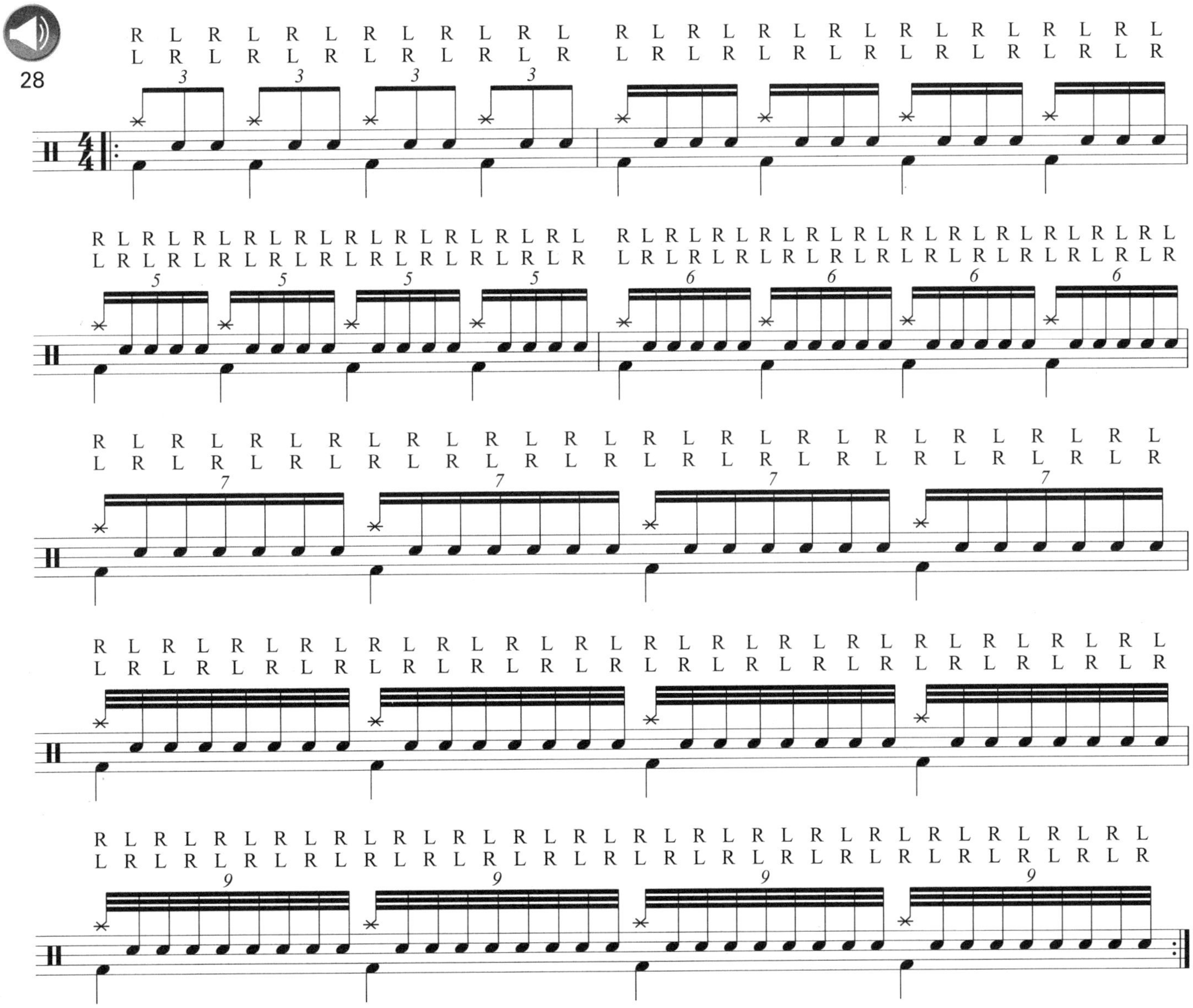

It would also be a good idea to try the previous exercise with a variety of sticking patterns, as in the following example.

Once you can play the previous exercise, mix and match the rhythms. Here's just one example:

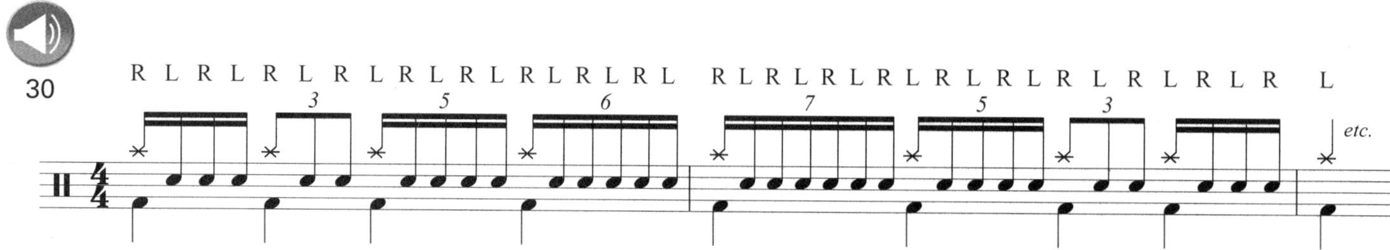

Now, go for a similar effect without worrying about the actual rhythmic groupings you are playing. Set your metronome to a moderate tempo and just start moving your hands, locking the bass drum in with the metronome pulse and hitting a crash or ride cymbal with whichever hand lands on the beat at a given time. (You don't necessarily have to hit a cymbal, though; you could just play an accent on the snare drum or hit a tom-tom.) Let your hands speed up and slow down as you go along. Eventually, instead of hitting every quarter note, just hit half notes or even whole notes.

Now you're ready to incorporate more freedom into your fills and solos. The next time you are tempted to play this:

...try something like this instead (don't worry about the specific rhythmic groupings; just go for the effect):

Everything doesn't have to be hand-to-hand. Throw in some flams...

...or play double strokes here and there (you can subdivide some of the notes using double strokes, as shown below):

Now, we're into the duality of subdivision and placement versus being free enough on another level to let our hands move in such a way as to create a burst or flurry of notes. It's an exciting way to play and gives the music more character. This works as an accompaniment as well as a soloistic device. Please refer to the end of Chapter 14 where I write, "During the drum solo section of this tune ["Three Quarter Molly"], I opted to eschew or avoid most of the downbeats or resolution (destination) points suggested by the form of the vamp. I felt that this brought my drumming closer than ever before to that of my drumming heroes." Audio Track 36 mirrors some of the previous note flurries.

Counterpoint and Comping

When you're practicing and have a time thing going—whether it's straight-eighth note or jazz—set up a dialogue between the bass drum and snare drum, or between the snare drum and hi-hat. Free up those elements of the kit from any traditional type of timekeeping, and while the time is going on the ride cymbal, explore what kind of dialogue you can have between the snare drum and bass drum.

You could think of it like:

31

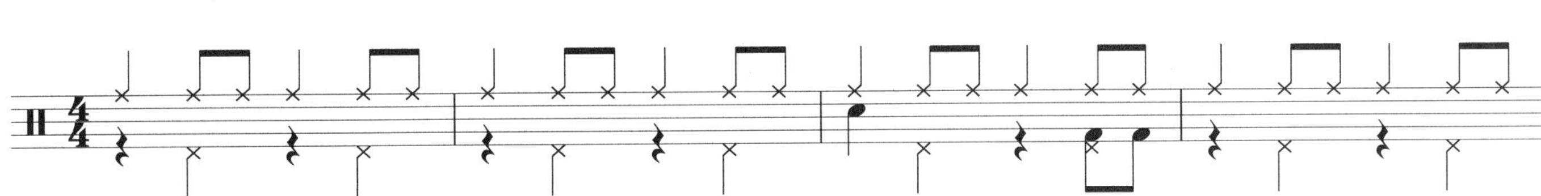

That's kind of a silly example, but you get the idea. If you can create a conversational quality within your own instrument, you can certainly create it within a band. How does that fit with comping? Are you accompanying or complementing what the other musicians are saying at that moment, or are you chattering away by yourself too much?

This also addresses the question of how to complement without merely "Mickey Mousing" what someone else plays. When the question is "Did ya happen to see the T.V.?" the answer is not "Did ya happen to see the T.V." By practicing questions and answers with yourself, say between bass and snare, you can learn to apply the same idea when you accompany a soloist or trade fours; it's a conversational approach.

Gary Burton says that when you comp, you are responding to the soloist as though he were talking and you were saying things like, "Oh yeah? Then, what happened? Wow! Tell me more." Of course, sometimes your job might be to interject "That's all fine and good, BUT..."

Continuing the analogy, it's good to remember your "manners." If a person walks into the room and starts talking, perhaps you should not start talking at the same time.

When you get into comping, unless you're playing some kind of a specific beat or shuffle-type rhythm, it shouldn't be repetitive. So, your ideas ought to take place over a longer period of time.

The Comping Game: "Don't Be a Jerk!"

The knee jerk is a common diagnostic tool used in medicine—that reflex tested by the doctor tapping just below the knee, which causes the lower leg to suddenly jerk forward. This has become such a common procedure and occurrence that it has "given rise to the adjective 'knee-jerk' as in a knee-jerk reaction. Knee-jerk in this figurative sense means 'readily predictable to the point of being automatic.' It often has a negative connotation and conveys the idea of an all-too-hasty, impulsive, irrational response based on a preset idea. For example, a dictator's knee-jerk response to a democratic movement is to suppress it."[5]

This concept could easily be applied to the musician who reacts automatically or without thinking when playing in an ensemble setting—more specifically, a drummer who comps or otherwise embellishes the act of timekeeping with rhythmic choices that are not so carefully chosen as much as played out of habit, muscle, or otherwise. Muscle habit is deadly to the creative enterprise, yet so easy to put into play time and time again. And the drummers who do this are the same ones who complain or admit that they've reached a creative wall in one situation or another (or across the board).

I've encountered this in my own playing, and I see and hear it in the playing of my students at USC and wherever I travel. I decided to combat this malady with a bit of creative fun/play: Welcome to **The Comping Game**.

The rules of the Comping Game are simple (but *very important* to follow!).

A. The ride cymbal may NOT change from its ride pattern of:

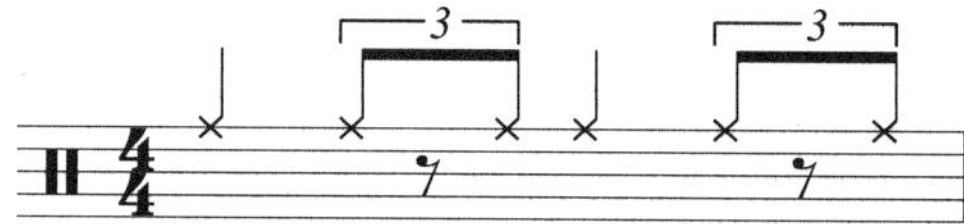

B. The hi-hat may NOT change from sounding on beats 2 and 4 as played by the foot.

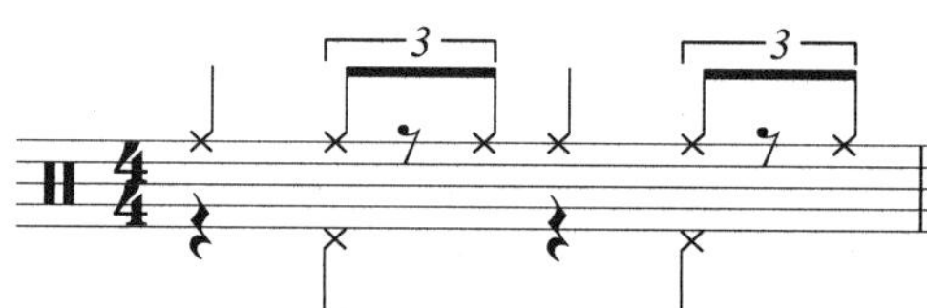

C. Each level of play's rule must be adhered to!

D. A "sameness" detector algorithm should be activated in your brain or the student's brain; the goal is to compose and be creative!

E. Dynamics MUST be varied!

F. Tempos MUST be varied!

G. Song choices must also change.

OK, here it goes: Level 1. The snare drum may be played ONE HIT and may NOT be played again until the bass drum is played for ONE HIT, and then the snare drum may be played again for one hit, etc. Simply alternating as an automaton follows the rules but defeats the purpose of the game.

---

5 medicine.en-academic.com/4561/Knee_jerk

Try this first with a 12-bar blues—for example, "Billie's Bounce."

The purpose of the game is to follow the rules and to use dynamics, space, and your ears—to be musical!

Now that you've successfully completed Level 1, let's try Level 2: two snare hits, followed by one bass drum hit, etc. Play these note choices as isolated events, and then try them as combos! Soon, you will discover new combinations and, dare I say, even new licks as you navigate these improvisational game waters.

Here is a complete list of the sequential note choice MENU, or RULES:

- Level 1: one snare, one kick
- Level 2: two snares, one kick
- Level 3: one snare, two kicks
- Level 4: two snares, two kicks
- Level 5: three snares, one kick
- Level 6: one snare, three kicks
- Level 7: three snares, two kicks
- Level 8: two snares, three kicks
- Level 9: three snares, three kicks
- Level 10: PLAY WHAT YOU'D LIKE TO HEAR!

The pedantic nature of the rules has a payoff, just like any good rules to any good game. Ingenuity and skill result in a winning combination when playing a game; we don't want to leave success up to the whims of Lady Luck alone (whether or not she is our muse). Seriously, this bit of creative play forces the musical drummer to become specific in his or her choices when it comes to improvising on the drumset in a timekeeping role. What a gift we all have! To compose as we play! And it's as easy as Levels 1, 2, 3 (4, 5, 6, 7, 8, 9, and 10).

Remember to vary the tempos, song forms and, most of all, dynamics when playing these new combinations. For example: in addition to the 12-bar blues form, practice (play the game) on such song forms as "Oleo" ("Rhythm Changes") and/or "All the Things You Are"; the extended forms will change the pacing of your rhythms and note choices. Obviously, a slow tempo will bring out different results than a medium tune or an up-tempo tune, etc. Also, keep in mind the value of breathing and inserting space into the musical proceedings, whatever the tempo. I encourage the use of space between the notes; often, the more space the better. Drummers do not need to doggie-paddle their way throughout a solo accompaniment, tune, an entire set, night, or their drumming lives.

I hope that the reader's knee-jerk response to this game will be to go practice—and swing. And have fun!

A Final Thought for This Chapter

One night, while playing with guitarist John Abercrombie and pianist Marc Copland, I had a revelation. In an epiphany,[6] I became aware of something I was doing that had to do with phrasing and barlines. Normally, as the music grows, develops, and swells towards a climax or a point of resolution, the drummer will usually accompany that build-up until the peak is reached, punctuating that moment with a cymbal crash or other drumming exclamation and then continuing with the next part of the song (perhaps switching to another cymbal at a softer dynamic for the next phrase of the solo, or the next soloist). Instead, I was anticipating the moment of resolution several bars earlier, not going along with the rest of the ensemble during their improvisatory build-up and foray; rather, I was already there when they arrived...

Surprise! This is what I imagine three-dimensional music to be like.

6 a. A sudden manifestation of the essence or meaning of something. b. A comprehension or perception of reality by means of a sudden intuitive realization.—*American Heritage Dictionary*.

CHAPTER 7

THE TEACHER/STUDENT RELATIONSHIP

"I've never known a musician who regretted being one. Whatever deceptions life may have in store for you, music itself is never going to let you down."

—Virgil Thompson,
commencement address at the New England Conservatory of Music

From the Student's Perspective...

I've wanted to be a jazz drummer for about as long as I can remember. And I've always been lucky to have the support of my parents and family, which came in the form of love and encouragement, as well as in their providing me access to some wonderful instruction.

YOUTH AND MASTER — Famous band leader, Stan Kenton, seems to highly approve of the playing of 7-year-old Peter Erskine of Linwood, above, who this week is attending Kenton's third annual music clinic at Indiana University. Son of Dr. and Mrs. F. A. Erskine, young Peter has been playing drums since he was five.

My first teacher, a fine drummer by the name of Johnny Civera, taught me how to hold the sticks, how to read, and the beginnings of how to play the drums with a band. At the summer Stan Kenton jazz camps that I used to attend, I was fortunate enough to receive instruction from such drummers as Louis Hayes, Charlie Perry, and Alan Dawson.

When Kenton told my father that he should contact a Professor George Gaber at Indiana University, Dad did so with, as usual, great determination and enthusiasm. Gaber's connection to Kenton was that he had recorded with Stan, playing timpani on the album *Cuban Fire*. He also had a reputation for having one of the finest percussion departments in the world (as part of the School of Music, Indiana University, Bloomington).

Mr. Gaber came to our family's house in New Jersey, at the invitation of my father, while he was visiting the East Coast on some other business. I was ten years old at the time. I knew that I was in the presence of a very important man. His warmth, congeniality, and genuine excitement for things percussive caused me to like him right away. I played for him, and he very kindly allowed for the possibility of my studying with him in the future.

A few months later, I took my first lesson from Mr. Gaber while in Indiana at a summer music camp. He instructed me to play a snare drum etude on the practice pad and to not play any of it correctly—to do so otherwise would result in his walking over to the pad and hitting me with a drumstick. "Excuse me?" I asked. "You heard me," he answered: "I want you to play that piece of music, but if you play any of it correctly or as written, you're going to get hit with a drumstick. Hard. Now play it." I glanced over at my mother who was present at the lesson, and she had a puzzled if not horrified look on her face, as if to say, "Who is this madman?" But I did as instructed and played the snare drum etude on the practice pad, playing the notes upside down and completely out of rhythm, etc., rendering the piece of music unrecognizable.

When I felt that I had done this long enough, I stopped and Gaber then took a satisfied puff on his cigar, said "Good," and continued: "Now, I want you to go over to that window, look outside and tell me what you see." I followed these instructions, and he prompted me while I was at the window, "Is the sun still shining? Are there clouds up in the sky? The trees are still there, it seems like the Earth is still spinning, right?" My mother was smiling now, getting the point of where Professor Gaber was going. "Now, come back to the practice pad." I did as he instructed. "You just played that snare drum piece as badly as it will ever be played. In fact, it could not be played any worse than how you played it. And yet, what happened? Absolutely nothing. Now, let's begin..."

Now, if THAT'S not a life lesson, then I don't know what is.

Peter's first meeting with George Gaber.

Peter's mom observing her son's lesson with Gaber.

Gaber then encouraged me to attend the Interlochen Arts Academy in Michigan for high school. I was to enjoy the study of both classical and jazz percussion. All of that time, I carried my trusty lesson book with me, which contained Mr. Gaber's advice for any drummer's most valuable assets (along with the ears): the hands. Mr. Gaber taught me that all drumming is made up of three basic strokes:

1. The single stroke
2. The double stroke
3. The flam

I worked on essential drumming rudiments such as flams, paradiddles, double-stroke rolls (5-stroke, 7-stroke, 9-stroke, etc.), and ruffs—rudiments that every drummer should be able to play. I recommend practicing on a practice pad. The things that Gaber would watch out for are the same things that I'll pass on to you: Strive for evenness in both hands regarding stick height, stick angle, and sound. Play relaxed, and practice at different tempos and dynamic levels. You could also practice these rudiments on the drumset between the snare and toms (perhaps over a bass drum/hi-hat ostinato) to increase your proficiency in moving around the kit, as discussed in the previous chapter.

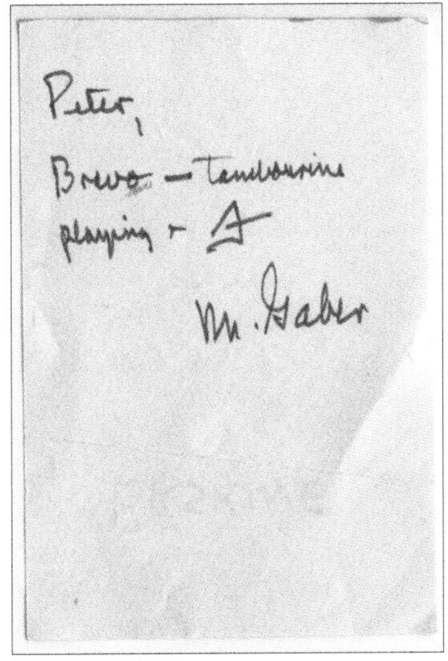

Peter,
Bravo — tambourine
playing — A
Mr. Gaber

Mr. Gaber taught me many things during our intermittent years of study—some of which have more and more meaning as I become older. Much of his advice concerned music and was to the point. While I did not receive too much specific instruction in jazz drumming per se, his pedagogy had more universal musical applications. For example, I had a tendency to hit the instrument too hard, pounding the sound into the drum (or whatever percussion instrument), as opposed to bringing, or pulling, the sound out of the instrument. What makes a great percussionist is his or her touch—the ability to walk up to a concert bass drum, triangle, cymbal, or tom-tom and get a beautiful sound from it. That is our art (as well as the way we observe the spaces between the notes!). We explored touch on many different percussion instruments: timpani, xylophone, marimba, snare drum, temple blocks, gongs, and cymbals, as well as more esoteric instruments like brake drums, caxixi, sleighbells, guiro, and the thunder drum. When he was pleased with something we played in a concert, he let us know by pinning notes to the bulletin board outside his door.

The other important lessons I remember, and that serve me well, include Mr. Gaber's philosophy that there would always be "that kid with the purple drumsticks." In other words, somebody fast and hot and impressive will always come along in the drum scene, and so a drummer had better find his or her own lasting musical values to sustain and nourish an artistic and playing career. That is to say, keep yourself centered and always answer that which music begs and demands from all of us: to be musical.

And in building a career, when the telephone starts to ring more and more, he taught me to never be afraid to say no to work, especially if it would interfere with family life. Keep priorities straight. For me, his advice has proven most sage; my family is everything for me. I think that our strength comes from our loved ones, as well as from inside of us. (Another important teacher, Joe Zawinul, told me that I would start to really play the drums once I had my own child, and I must admit, he was right.)

George Gaber taught me the value of appreciating the entire universe of knowledge—things percussion and otherwise. May I have his sense of humanity and universality into my golden years! I'll quote from a letter Mr. Gaber once wrote me: "Let me remind you that the 'just jazz' drummers have been with us always, and the unusual, curious, experimental, gifted, and professional drummers have always been with us too. The versatile drummers from the turn of this century played styles and universal concepts with panache while others played narrowly and poorly." In other words, whatever your style, learn from the world of music. It is rich with sound and experience!

Professor Gaber would prove to be a lifelong friend, a man whose wisdom, advice, and love for music has accompanied me every day and in most every circumstance, musical or otherwise. He's always with me in word, thought, musical choice, or touch. Professionalism was his calling, musicality his ethos, compassion and laughter his response to life's challenges. His advice was as sharp as his wit. Gaber would say of fame: "That, plus 50 cents, will get you a ride on any subway in New York." The train costs more now, but his advice is still true.

In 2006, I rented a car after a gig in Missouri and drove eight-plus hours on a rainy Sunday to my alma mater, IU, where there would be a celebration of my professor's 90th birthday. George Gaber still meant the world to me. I spoke during dinner to the crowd of former students, ad-libbing as jazz musicians love to do. I found myself talking about his sense of humanity and the love he taught for music, for being musical, and for being ethical. He returned the compliment during dessert by saying that I had "Gladstone hands," and he reminded me that our two-year course of study during my university years centered around my wish for him to "work on my hands." We approached all percussion instruments from the point of view of *tone*. It took quite a few years for his lessons to sink in and take root. My entire drumming approach was nurtured and shaped by the generous wisdom and wealth of experience of Professor George Gaber. His words still resonate and provide useful guidance.

As I finished editing the manuscript of the first edition of this book in December 1997, I was glad to report that George Gaber and I were still corresponding about matters both musical and philosophical. When I learned that my professor, mentor, and friend of more than 40 years had passed away in 2007 at the age of 91, I was asked to sum up my feelings for him in four short lines of text for *The New York Times*. I wrote:

"GG taught his students well.

Professionalism, musicality,

compassion & laughter:

his calling, ethos & way of life."

He shall be missed.

From the Teacher's Perspective...

Not only have I taken quite a few drum lessons in my life, I've also given quite a few. The following observations are geared more toward teachers, but will hopefully prove helpful to students as well as teachers. I also hope to challenge some existing methodologies.

Peter with students at the Interlochen Arts Camp.

Private Lessons

The students who come to me for instruction are, in most cases, drummers who have been playing for some time. They usually come for just a lesson or two, due to my schedule as well as my relatively high fee. (I do have a couple of students who come regularly, however.) For many of these players, I function as a diagnostician as much as an instructor. My ability to listen critically has been nurtured by years of "self-analysis" in recording studios, concert halls, and jazz clubs (along with plenty of free advice given by bandmates!).

I've also had the opportunity to observe young, developing drummers for most of my professional life. When I joined the Stan Kenton Orchestra in 1972 at age eighteen, I not only played the music on the gig each night but also taught it during the day at clinics and summer camps.

During a lesson, I try to provide advice and feedback that is relevant and in concentrated form. This is important because there is no luxury of time over repeated visits and short-term goal preparations by the student—a process with values and advantages that I respect, incidentally.

By either method, I think it vital that the teacher ask and ascertain the drummer's goals—his or her dreams, if you will—at the beginning of the study relationship. A drum book or series of exercises does not an education make. While there are common nuts and bolts with which we all must wrestle, a little consideration of each drummer's aspirations will help focus the direction of our instruction. I require that all my students be aware that being musical (and making the music feel as good as possible) is their first responsibility—along with self-improvement.

I utilize audio and video technology when teaching so as to document the lesson by recording it, often using that recording for instant review and analysis. When first listening to something just played, the tendency is to hear it "drumistically" (i.e., as a drummer). That's fine and good as far as it goes, which is to say it's pretty narrow and self-limiting. Just as an infant is mainly concerned by its immediate wants, needs, and surroundings, immature or self-centered musicians will only hear what they did in terms of their own execution of the drumming act, ignoring its impact on the rest of the ensemble.

By way of example, imagine a student playing 4/4 time along with an imaginary rhythm section with soloist. The tempo should be medium and the song should be a mutually agreed-upon, recognizable piece so that the form may be observed. The "tape is rolling," the tune is counted off, and the music begins. Let two or three choruses go by, stop the student (with an encouraging word), go back to the beginning of the file, and listen together in silence.

Adherence to tempo and form will be apparent right away. How about dynamic balance on the kit (snare drum too loud, etc.)? If any fills were played, the student may register delight or displeasure at how they were performed... and so on. Ask the student what he or she liked or didn't like about what was just heard. There will be one level of self-awareness.

Now, rewind the performance again and have the student listen to the drumming as though he or she is the bass player or piano player. (I even have my students put their hands in imaginary bass-playing or piano-playing positions.) Suddenly, a whole new level of awareness opens up. Students will realize that "the drums are too busy... there's no room for the piano to comp... there's not enough flow," and the like. It's one of those gratifying "light bulb" moments in teaching and learning. Help students graduate from listening drumistically to listening the way that other members of the group hear the drums. In other words, drummers should listen to what they do as musicians.

Now, discuss with the student what to play while accompanying other musicians, which is pretty much a drummer's stock in trade! Of course, it is all the more instructive if you (the teacher) can actually sit down and play whatever it is you're talking about.

It's essential to get drummers to think of ways to contribute compositionally to the progression of any piece of music. What is played is important—every big and little bit of it. Making each note count for more and being aware of its place in the big picture is my own playing and teaching mission. I encourage all teachers to prioritize their educational and playing agendas; I suggest that stressing musicality *en toto* be *prima facie*, however!

Develop a listening program for both teacher and student. If the focus is jazz, the program needs a selective history of styles that goes back before the late 1970s and early 1980s, please! I refer to mainstream bebop drummers as my starting point for exemplifying good, straight-ahead, swinging drumming: recordings of Philly Joe Jones (with Sonny Rollins and/or Miles Davis), Art Blakey, Max Roach, Kenny Clarke, Roy Haynes, Louis Hayes (with Cannonball Adderley—that was a swinging band!), Elvin Jones, Buddy Rich, Tony Williams, Mel Lewis, Louie Bellson, Jack DeJohnette, et al. It's also illuminating and essential to listen to recordings of such drummers as "Papa" Jo Jones (how he swung the Basie band with just his hi-hats!), Baby Dodds, Big Sid Catlett, Dave Tough, and Tiny Kahn (with apologies for any drummers left out). If teaching includes pop, rock, samba, or other styles, then listen to exemplary recordings of those types of music along with the students. It's the best way to hear something done right.

Those concepts should be enough, but here are some "nuts and bolts" items to consider:

1. **Student posture, breathing, and the amount of movement in arms, wrists, fingers, and legs.** There is usually too much movement for the stroke(s) being played. Concentrate on focus and being centered. If necessary, isolate the movement of limbs to weed out non-productive playing habits. Basic independence/coordination exercises are useful; be sure to stress the importance of swinging and always sounding musical.
2. **Self-awareness.** Urge students to practice in front of a mirror (or use a video camera, smartphone, etc.). They should record their practice sessions and rehearsals. Self-awareness is the key.

3. **Size and setup of the kit.** First, every part of the drumkit should be easy enough to reach so the drummer can pivot and be in playing (striking) position while comfortably seated with arms down by the sides and shoulders relaxed.

   Second, every drummer should periodically reduce the number of elements in the drumkit setup to develop a better sense of focus and confidence. Too many drums or cymbals can lead to a distracted approach to timekeeping. After all, it's tempting to want to hit everything that's in front of you. Also, be careful how you use certain "effects" cymbals—especially China types, which are relatively dry and percussive—as they can be disruptive in terms of the time feel. Too often, drummers are being clever or hyperactive instead of developing a flow to their music.

   When I was in college, Professor Gaber suggested that I use a stripped-down drumkit (bass drum, hi-hat, snare drum, cymbal) for occasional gigs. I, however, wanted to have all my "trappings" for every performance (to be a hot-shot).

   Over twenty years later, I finally tried the idea big time by taking only two cymbals and hi-hats to Europe for a month-long tour with Kenny Wheeler. (This after watching a video of the Miles Davis band circa 1964 with Tony Williams playing with only two cymbals.) May the patron saints of Zildjian forgive me—less was decidedly more! I use many different cymbals for different applications, especially some recordings, but this was a refreshing education in actually playing a cymbal as an instrument, developing a relationship with it—not just hitting one of many articles in front of me, around me, above me, etc. Extend this notion to the number of tom-toms in a kit.
4. **Tempos.** Practice things slow and fast, not just at a medium tempo. Spend some time on whole notes.
5. **Creativity.** Challenge students to play what they've never played before. Licks are against the law here. The use of an ostinato is a good idea; a drum machine or sequencer can provide this, or the students can come up with simple patterns of their own with the bass drum and hi-hat, and compose drum melodies and rhythms on the tom-toms, snare, and cymbals. I sometimes say to my students, "Wouldn't it be great after a concert to hear someone whistling or humming parts of the drum solo you just played?" It begs the question, "Are we musicians or just a collection of rudimental strokes/drum-flavor-of-the-month licks?"
6. **Balance and open-mindedness.** Good drumming and music ought to be life-affirming aesthetic activities. I encourage you and your students to enjoy the path of discovery. And above all else, make it funky!

USC

I have been teaching drums at the University of Southern California's Thornton School of Music since 2002. We teach beginning drumset as part of a degree requirement: All popular music performance majors are required to master basic drumming techniques and drumset beats. We teach eight students at a time in a drum lab setup, much like an electronic keyboard lab setup where the instructor has a headset and communicates with each student individually or collectively. This class is one of the most popular music courses at USC. In one semester's time, enrollment grew from sixteen to sixty-four students, and we've added more sections or class times every year. The history of contemporary music is very intertwined with the development of the drumset and drumbeats, and we're teaching all of that.

My private students are all great—excellent players and inquisitive students. The school's jazz department is a strong magnet, and it has been attracting some terrific players. I asked one of them once why a particular recording was so good (the recording in question was Keith Jarrett's "Common Mama" on the album *Expectations* with Paul Motian playing drums in a hypnotic and compellingly modern way); "uncommon" would be a word for it. But my student does me one better: "It's great because Paul Motian is letting the music do all of the work." I'm getting paid to teach, but I feel as though I'm the one who's learning.

However, I can get impatient with some of my students. I say, "Your drumming is fine; you're doing all the right drumming stuff. And I'm sick of drumming like that." Let's make some music, and don't just play what you're used to playing. Don't keep reacting the way you always react because when any instrumentalists—but drummers, especially—seem to start feeling uncomfortable, they start sounding very much like the way they did in high school. You know, "Oh man, what am I going to do?" You can get beyond that; you don't have to fall back on the stuff you know. Don't play what you know; play what you don't know."

While on the road in Europe, I wrote a letter to my university students at the Thornton School of Music that chronicled my sense of a change in my own playing over the years—an arrival of sorts. I was feeling a bit guilty for being on the road and not on campus!

> "Ex Libris" means "from the library of." There are many words whose first two letters are "ex": excellence, excess, extra, extravagance, and expedience. And it would seem that much of our energies are expended towards adding one or another of these quantities to our "libraries." It's fair to observe that all of us are looking for more technique, more vocabulary, more acknowledgement, more playing opportunities, more fame, more money, more excitement, and so on. This is a natural and necessary part of the learning experience.
>
> But something happens once we expand our point of view (otherwise known as getting older and/or wiser): We begin to yearn for less. We look for cleaner lines, simpler reasons, more obvious truths, and less-complicated scenarios. Fewer notes (accompanied by better choices). The old "less is more" idea—the only caveat being that the "less" is more informed. In any event, the creation of art becomes more of a reductive exercise.
>
> "The most important part of a pencil is the eraser," composer Vince Mendoza told me.
>
> The only person who expressed this better, perhaps, would be Michelangelo (Michelangelo di Lodovico Buonarroti Simoni, 1475–1564), the Italian sculptor, painter, architect, and poet of the High Renaissance period. As a sculptor, whose medium was a block of marble, he created art by the reduction or taking away from the whole in order to express his vision.
>
> Look at the photo of his Pietà—which was carved from one piece of marble—and think about that.

An extended tour provided me with multiples of playing experiences and situations: Being the drummer in a symphony orchestra in London, and then performing a solo drumset performance at a chops-fest gig in Spain, followed by a trio tour throughout Italy that included a stop in Rome where I had the occasion to visit the Vatican and marvel at the Pietà in person. What an experience! (I first saw this magnificent sculpture as a ten-year-old boy in 1964, when it was brought to the New York World's Fair by the Vatican.)

If the sculptor does not take away enough marble, then the nose is too big. On the other hand, if they take away too much marble, then the nose is too small. There's not a lot of margin for error—three-dimensional excellence that has provided inspiration to an infinite number of persons. Such is the power of art.

And such is the potential in each of your hands. Music can have the same impact and importance when it reaches the ears and hearts and minds of your audience. And it can give each one of you a glimpse into the infinite expanse of God, or Nature, or Mother Earth, or however you deem to term that which is greater than us.

Everyone can gaze at the stars at night and enjoy their sparkling brilliance. But if we want to know more about a star or planet, then we will turn to the telescope, and this is where *focus* comes into play. I submit that the same can be said for expanding the depth and scope of your playing; some focus is required. I am confident that you will begin to find that by being more specific and intentional, your compositional abilities will continue to grow as much as they will become a natural extension of your musical mind, hands, and feet.

I forgot to mention the master classes I have been presenting (two in London, one in Geneva, another in Milan, a three-hour class in Paris, and an upcoming workshop in Basel). Part of the reason I enjoy teaching is because of how much I learn in the process—which, in turns allows me to be a more informed teacher. This is the process I now find myself in.

I am looking forward to sharing some of the music made with Alan Pasqua and Darek Oles during this trip—hopefully by means of a new live album. We managed to reach a pretty high level of expression, I like to think. The trick was not just in playing less. Finding the balance between less and more was the ultimate game, and we managed to get the nose just right a few times.

I also sent that letter to my oldest and closest friend from high school. Here is his reply:

"Peter Erskine, I've just read your mail to your students. Thanks for sending it to me. I paid attention in your letter... knowing 'a thing' had happened. That was super clear. Speaking this to your students is courageous and real and it is inspirational. What happened. No question mark. I'll take my time to attempt to accurately speak to what's happened to you... possibly. It may be like continuing to play the lottery or waiting for that bus that's supposed to come but doesn't. And then... the bus comes or your numbers hit. You had no control. It happens. You take the bus. You are left with money you didn't have before. Where are you going and how to spend that money? Getting the bus and having the money have nothing to do with it, of course.

"You just experienced *The Wizard of Oz* effect: 'If I ever go looking for my heart's desire again, I won't look any farther than my own backyard, because if it isn't there, I never really lost it to begin with.' I suggest that what happened to you is a thing that's held itself in you waiting for you to find you. Frustrating? Maybe. But it happened. You finding you. Beautiful. Intense. Real. Real. It's real.... I really appreciate your letter to those lucky students and I consider myself one of them."

Sharing Secrets

One night, while celebrating the end of a successful day of teaching at the TMEA convention in San Antonio by dining on some fine Tex-Mex cuisine, one of my companions at the table (who is not a drummer but is married to a female percussionist) commented that the world of drumming seemed quite unique. His reason? "This is the only line of work I can think of where people who are competing for the same job willingly get together to share their trade secrets." To be honest, I had never really thought of it in quite that same fashion, but it does seem painfully obvious. Musicians, especially drummers, do seem to enjoy camaraderie and a confidence that is unlike most any other endeavor imaginable. Confidence seems to come from knowledge. Knowledge comes from our being taught well. Teaching our children well means that we direct our resources towards education *now* so as to avoid having to fix bigger societal problems later.

CHAPTER 8

MY MANNE, SHELLY

Shelly Manne at soundcheck, Aurex Jazz Festival, Tokyo, Japan, 1980.
Photo by Peter Erskine.

Shelly Manne was one of my first drum heroes, and he remains a hero to this day. A swinging drummer in any context, he personified eclecticism while remaining a singularly unique musician. Shelly could do it all.

Since the term "lick" carries negative connotations when it comes to discussing creativity, I'd like to focus this chapter on a rhythmic and sticking pattern that might best be termed a "device." And as devices are useful to have in one's toolbox, I hope you'll be inspired to add this to your bag of tricks.

This triplet-based device works equally well for comping as it does for soloing (especially when trading fours, eights, etc.). Many drummers will recognize this as something that both Philly Joe Jones and Shelly Manne employed. Here is the device on its own with two different starting points:

The dynamic range of this device is somewhat limited in the sense that it is not a power tool. The triplets are played by the hands and not the feet, so it's already lighter than most hand/foot combinations. And because it is most commonly played on the ride area of the cymbal (not on the edge or bell), the texture and flow work really well together.

Here is the device in the context of time. I suggest you practice this on its own, and then incorporate it into your ride/time playing:

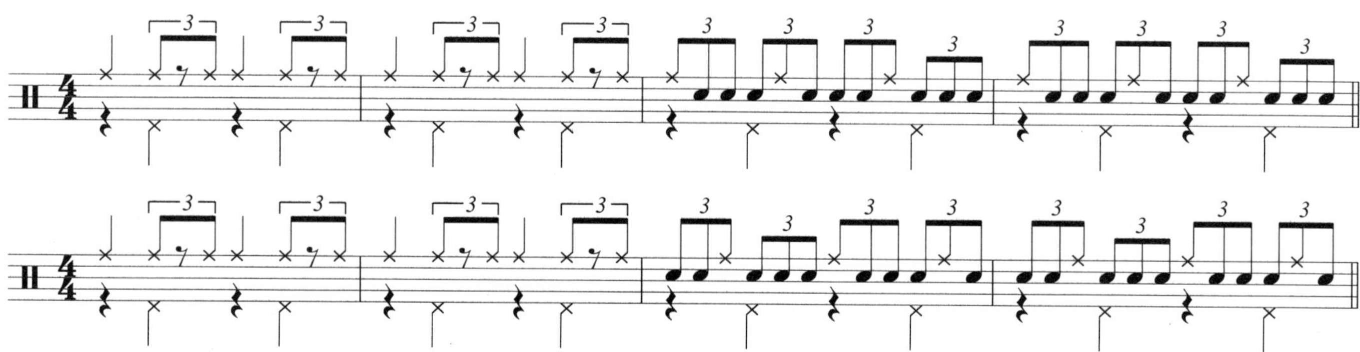

As with all things worth practicing, choose and use different tempos.

For listening reference, I'll suggest the following examples:

- On the Miles Davis recording of "The Serpent's Tooth" (from the album *Collector's Items*), he trades fours with Philly Joe Jones at 5:45 into the tune. (You can probably find the recording on YouTube.)

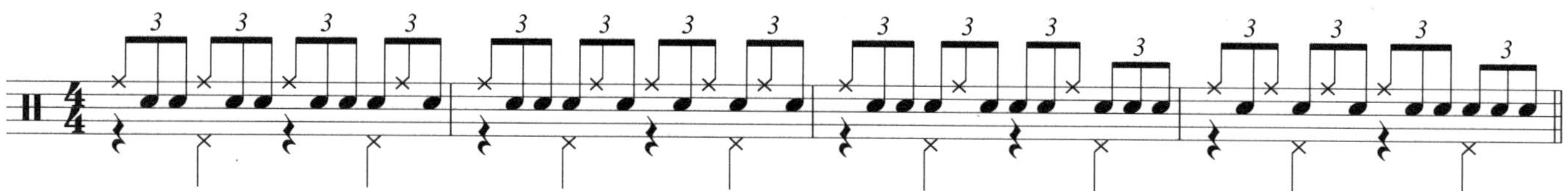

- On the recording of "Moose the Mooche" by Shelly Manne and His Men, Shelly trades phrases at 5:39 into the tune. (You can probably find the recording on YouTube.)

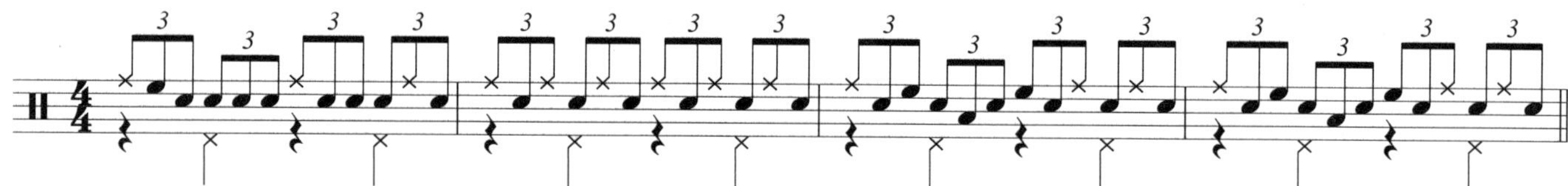

Note that both Shelly and Philly Joe often simply alternated triplets between the snare and cymbal.

- Peter Erskine, "The Honeymoon" (I employ this device while playing time and comping, as well as during my trades with the song's composer, bassist Darek Oles).

3: "The Honeymoon"

In any event, this is a device that's easy to play, plus easy to make sound and feel good.

But wait, there's more.

While demonstrating this to one of my students at the Thornton School of Music at USC, I chanced upon this happy discovery—altering the sticking from this:

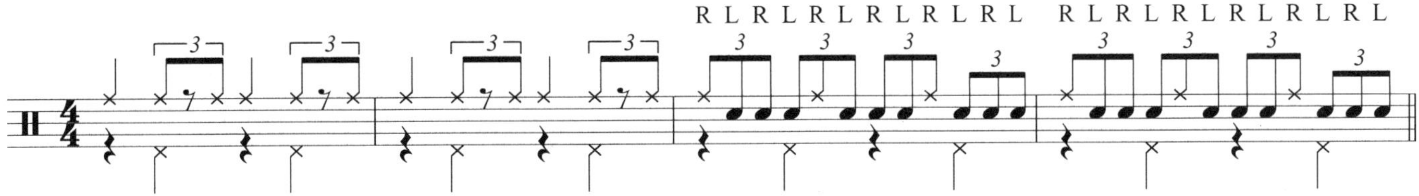

...to this:

This allows for some pretty high-level "word play" (also known as polyrhythmic sophistication) without the drummer needing to think too much about it while playing.

I'll repeat that: WITHOUT THE DRUMMER NEEDING TO THINK TOO MUCH ABOUT IT WHILE PLAYING.

Because: ISN'T THAT THE WHOLE POINT?

As always, use your ears to achieve the best balance, which in turn will achieve the best flow (or feel), which will result in the other musicians you're playing with perceiving your contributions to the music as being that much more valuable, desirable, and important. Any and all sticking variations should work.

All of which should result in more playing opportunities and greater creativity. And isn't *that* the whole point of why we do what we do?

One additional/built-in feature to this device is that the drummer need not end the playing of these triplets with a bass drum and cymbal accent, or "destination point." It comes and it goes.

Choose good heroes and do your best to honor them every day and in every way. And keep swinging, gang.

CHAPTER 9

MEETING A PIECE OF MUSIC FOR THE FIRST TIME

> *"Music is your own experience, your thoughts, your wisdom. If you don't live it, it won't come out of your horn."*
>
> —Charlie Parker

When meeting a piece of music for the first time (whether it's written or not), it is a good idea to be mindful of your manners. I think it's proper etiquette for you to take music's hand, give it a shake, look it straight in the eye and ask, "How are you?" I don't think you should immediately start telling it your problems ("Hi. My uncle's in a mental hospital, and my mother just ran off with the dry cleaner."). And you don't need to start by trying to impress the music with bragging, either ("I'm the baddest drummer to come down the pike since..."). Yet, how often are we guilty of musically inappropriate forwardness?

I am thinking of the many times that I have asked students to play something funky for me. What followed would be the gosh-darndest, most complicated, and least funky beat in the world. An attempt, on the surface, would be to try to utilize some of the more fascinating and tricky kinds of things that David Garibaldi, Steve Gadd, Dave Weckl, or Vinnie Colaiuta can play, but without any knowledge of where the backbeat should really go. There's also a lack of any awareness of a possible musical context outside of their own determined mind-set (suggesting, too, that there is a tendency when playing the drums "solo" or alone to do anything but that which is simple). So then I say, "Well, how about something funky?"

I pause as I write this and glance into the mirror. I don't see the world's greatest authority on funk staring back at me (and since the implied domain of this book is jazz drumming, I'm not going to worry about it now). But in this age of the Renaissance drummer, it is necessary to be able to play and meet a lot of different music on its own terms while still bringing something of ourselves to it. And, not surprisingly, what works for one style of music generally works for another. One could say, "The shortest distance between two points will always be a straight line."

So what's all this got to do with the price of drumsticks? In practical terms, you should always start off simply, with your ears wide open. That is, start by playing the best time you can. And consider full well the context of your playing situation. For example, when I go into a studio, sit down behind the drums, and see that I will be playing a funk (or some kind of straight eighth-note) chart, I start by playing the simplest of beats. Because my ears are open, and because the musical space is not all filled up by my ambitions, I can then hear what the rest of the rhythm section is trying to do—what kind of line the bassist is playing, what the rhythm guitar is doing, etc.

By starting simply, I've left open the possibility that this musical friendship can go someplace. Then, I can get a little more clever or intimate if I want to. It's the same with a piece of music that I play for the first time with any jazz group; by starting off simply, openly, and respectfully, I can then fully develop my relationship with the music.

Let me give you an example of how I approached and developed a beat for a particular piece of music. The first time I played the tune "Pools" with the band Steps Ahead (written by Don Grolnick and recorded on the album *Steps Ahead*), the rehearsal went something like this: Don started to play the tune on the piano, and I could hear the open nature of the composition—particularly a bass pattern that did not begin on the downbeat of the tune or, indeed, the bars. Without a bass ostinato or continuous pattern being played, it seemed obvious that the drums should provide some sort of a "constant." In other words, the drums had to be a "cushion" for the rest of the music. My first choice for a beat resembled this:

32

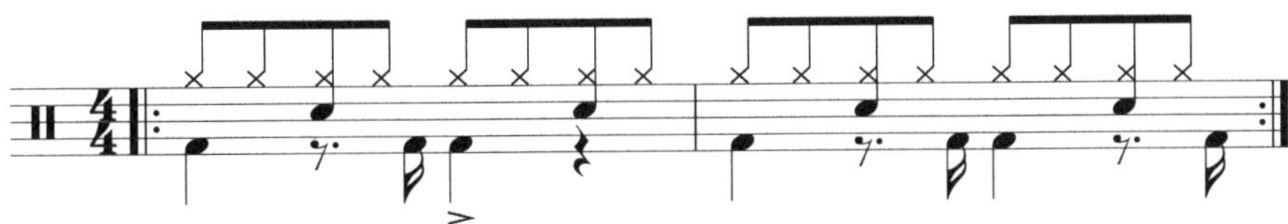

Sensing that the tune should use the quality of something different in terms of the drumbeat, I re-orchestrated that beat, getting more of a reggae-type, half-time feel (keeping my bass drum off the downbeats as well).

33

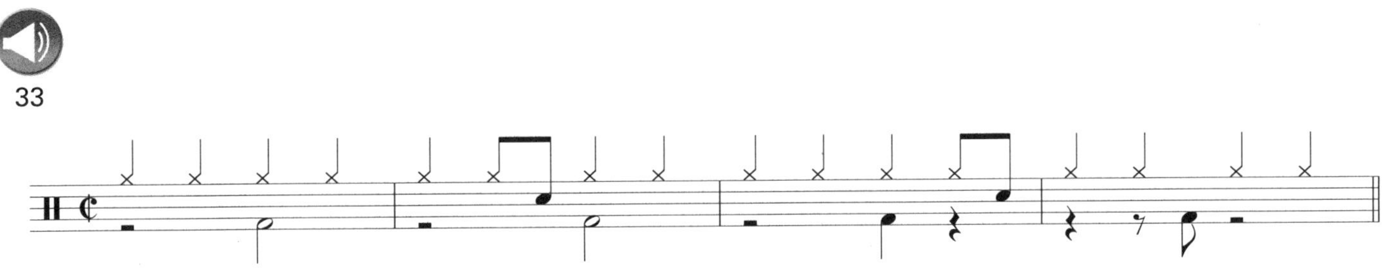

Something else was needed to develop the beat: a different hi-hat pattern. I could have played constant eighth notes on the hi-hat, but going along with the open nature of the tune, a more open hi-hat pattern seemed fitting.

34

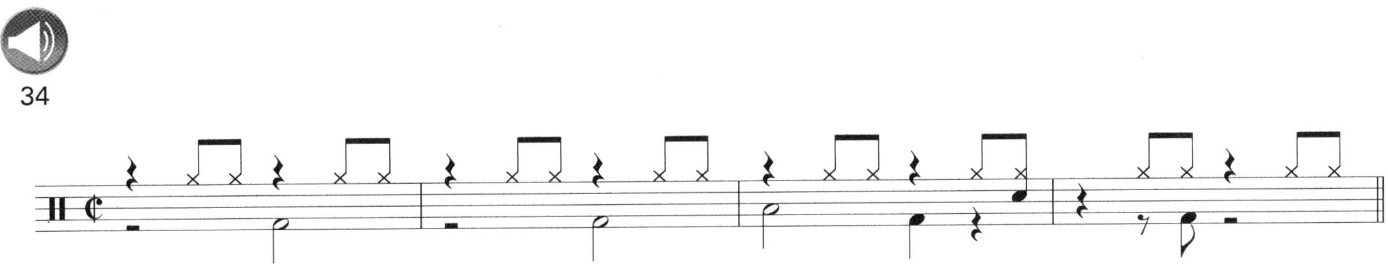

The hi-hat became the constant, along with the bass drum (more or less). Texturally, the beat is open. Conceptually, I can add the appropriate accents wherever I want, without detracting from the timekeeping (heard on the hi-hat and, oftentimes, the bass drum on beat 2). Thus, the beat is strong but not too busy. (A good drumbeat should be as solid as a mighty oak tree, while at the same time having the quality of sunlight or fresh air coming through its branches.)

The following sixteen bars are transcribed from "Pools." The pattern I played on the recording had a slight variation in the hi-hat part. In the previous example, the hi-hat part has a quarter rest followed by two eighth notes, repeated. On the recording, I played a quarter note followed by two eighth notes, repeated. However, I "ghosted" the quarter notes and accented the eighths, so the overall effect was the same.

35

When in doubt, play simply and not too busy. And always listen to the bass player, whose pattern will guide your feet and hands as to what to play. That being said, this beat, dating back to the early 1980s, is more intricate and busier than what I would choose to play today. The built-in clockwork would inform my intent, but the actual beat would be much more lean. To make an analogy, I prefer black T-shirts nowadays compared to the colorful, patterned shirts I wore as a young man. And that's just the way it's supposed to be!

One other point: While on tour with Steely Dan back in 1993, I was playing the "Purdie shuffle" beat used to such great effect on the tune "Babylon Sisters," and I had all of the ghost notes down to the last diddle—and when I heard a recording of one of the concerts, it felt *all wrong*. Why? Because I was focused on the frosting, not the cake. I had to go back and teach myself the essence of the beat for that song. 1–2–3–4. Yep, simple as that: the downbeat, followed by a backbeat, and so on. Then, adding the bits of color, subdivision, and nuance that give the beat its signature. It's always a good idea to return to basics in the middle of whatever you're doing. It keeps the music not only lean but more honest, too.

Learning Music for the Gig

One of the greatest pleasures you can receive from music is when you have the opportunity to play in a variety of settings. I count myself as having been very fortunate in that regard. If "variety is the spice of life," then I am living in a paradise of condiments and flavors. These various playing and stylistic possibilities are not only a source of enrichment for me; indeed, they constitute the bulk of my work as a freelance musician. In other words, one must be flexible and willing to learn and take chances in order to make a good living as a musician (and live a good life as a musician, I believe).

Here, then, are some practical tips and suggestions concerning your getting ready for that next gig (which is always just around the corner).

First, it is assumed that you can play a good, steady beat! Second, it's a good idea to have some sort of intimacy or awareness of the musical style that you're going to be playing. This calls for not only an understanding of the rhythmic subdivision that characterizes that style of music (i.e., "feel"), but also an idea of the type of sound that the music calls for. (This has to do with the tuning of your kit, relative sizes of the snare, toms, and bass drum, cymbal selection, etc.) It also helps if you actually like the music you are going to play! At any rate, keeping an open ear and mind helps.

Allow me to draw upon a personal experience to illustrate the process of learning the music for a gig. I was asked to play a short West Coast tour with singer Boz Scaggs during the summer of 1995. I was delighted to be offered the gig—although the job offer came as a bit of a surprise, as I don't tend to think of myself so much as an R&B player. I guessed that the call came about as a result of my having done a Steely Dan tour a couple of years prior.

I have always been a fan of Boz's music, though I must confess that I was not too familiar with his recordings other than *Silk Degrees*, which had the late, great Jeff Porcaro playing drums. As it turned out, except for the music from Boz's latest recording (with drum tracks by Ricky Fataar, an excellent drummer whose work I was not aware of until getting the record *Some Change*), Jeff had recorded just about all of the tunes that we would be playing live on tour. In addition, then, to getting to learn these tunes (an initial set list was comprised of twenty-six songs), I received an incredible education about the true mastery of Jeff Porcaro's drumming.

At the time that I received two cassettes brimming with songs yet-to-be-learned by me, I was on tour with my own trio in Europe, playing music of a decidedly different style and dynamic range! I wanted to concentrate on what I was doing at the moment, so I waited until my flight back home to Los Angeles (with Boz rehearsals looming ahead just a few days later) to actually listen to these tapes and start learning the songs. (So many tunes, so little time.) Needless to say, preparation is important in any gig, especially one in which the drummer has to provide the signature beat for each song. There can't be any question as to how the song goes once it is counted off—and the count-off is usually the drummer's responsibility, too! Since I didn't really know too many of these songs, I started taking notes while I listened to these tapes on the plane.

In addition to a portable cassette player and headphones, I had a book of music paper and a pencil. It's also a good idea to have a pocket metronome; the type with a "Tempo Set" function works best (i.e., one that enables the user to enter in a tempo by tapping the beat into the device). While today's smartphones offer a multitude of music-related apps, I still prefer to have a stand-alone metronome handy.

While listening, I took notes as to the basic drumbeat for each tune. Popular music usually has a "signature" beat for every song. What are the kick and snare playing? Is the hi-hat an eighth-note or sixteenth-note groove? Identifying each song's particular beat, I started compiling a "cheat sheet" of the song list.

As you can see, these notes are very basic. But they provided, at a glance, the necessary information I needed to confidently play these songs at rehearsal and at the gig. For example, I could tell at a glance that "Miss Sun" has the bass drum playing on beats 1 and 3, snare drum on beats 2 and 4 (that's almost a given in the genre), with the interesting hi-hat rhythm of offbeat eighth notes. The cheat sheet also showed me the beat for the bridge of the song, as well as the parenthetical snare drum embellishments that Jeff played on the original recording.

Once I had this starting-off place, I could then begin to really learn the tune by actually playing it with the band. When it comes to reading, I've always felt that a good pair of ears is better than a good set of eyes—even more so when learning a new piece of music without any actual charts to read from. In the case of the Boz gig, we (the rhythm section) decided to make some changes here and there to the music, like changing a 1-and-3 bass drum pattern to a "four-on-the-floor" beat (1–2–3–4). I took notes during rehearsal, revising information concerning beats, arrangements, etc. It's not necessary to write out complete charts of every song. Find your own method of shorthand that you can be comfortable with.

Percussionist Lenny Castro was extremely helpful in this regard. He is not only a great percussionist, but he also played this music with Jeff. I took his recommendations and advice eagerly—which brings me to another point. While it is essential to exude confidence from behind the kit, you must also be willing to take advice from other members or the leader as to the way a song might be rendered (also known as "check your hats and egos at the door").

Ultimately, you'll have to find your own balance between playing what the boss wants and playing what you sincerely feel the music needs. Hopefully, those two ideals will meet.

Most of all, you should allow the music to inform you as to what to play. It will always tell you honestly.

Once you have begun to interpret and play this music, your understanding of it will grow and grow. In the case of my doing this short tour with Boz Scaggs, my drumming evolved from an imitation of some of Jeff's playing (he was a great and gifted genius), to an actual true understanding of the feel and flow possible for each tune. In other words, I went from playing some of Jeff's beats and fills on the surface of the tune to playing those same rhythms deep within each moment of the song. This means playing everything as an essential part of the groove—finding the "pocket." The pocket is the heart and soul of music's meaning—particularly, the placement of the downbeat and backbeat. The subtle ornamentations (for example, the hi-hat and snare fills) complete the picture.

The tour was a terrific success. Boz's gracious compliment to me at the end of the tour was that he felt so comfortable singing his tunes because he had such a good "bed" to work from. This made me extremely happy because that let me know that I had done my job well.

That couple of hours' worth of listening and note-taking homework really paid off, not only during those crucial first moments of rehearsing the music, but during the gigs as well. I kept a copy of my "cheat sheet," photocopied/reduced and encased in laminated plastic—which any good copy shop can do—right by my drumkit during the entire tour. An attentive mind and pair of ears, along with a good memory (which comes from paying attention), paid off.

So whether it's rock 'n' roll, jazz, or a show, it's always a good idea to **be prepared**. And make it swing!

CHAPTER 10

INTROS

Scene: jam session, rehearsal, or gig.

Line: "Let's play 'Green Dolphin Street' ...and, drums, how about you play an intro?"

Spot Quiz:

A. Do you ask, "How long?"
B. Do you ask, "What tempo?"
C. Do you ask, "What kind of feel do you want?"
D. Do you play a solo?

Answer: *None of the above.*

Let's work our way backwards. An intro is NOT a solo. It is meant to function as a short bit of rhythmic storytelling that sets the time and feel and solves the problem of how to start the tune. In this sense, we are as much plumbers as we are storytellers or musicians. By this I mean, when we call a plumber to unclog the sink, we don't expect him or her to ask us how we'd like them to unclog it; we simply want it unclogged. That is, we want the problem solved. Good problem solvers are valued in any setting and in any organization (read: BAND).

Let's talk about feel. You should know the feel of the song, at least if it's a jazz standard. Otherwise, the person requesting the intro (usually the bandleader) should make mention of the style, perhaps going so far as snapping their fingers (that takes care of tempo). If you know the feel, and the tempo is being left to your discretion, then you'll be expected to handle that as well.

Now, "How long?" This takes us back to the beginning (or the end): An intro is not a solo. When in doubt, shorter is better than longer.

OK, so now that we've answered the Spot Quiz, what else do we need to know? Using "On Green Dolphin Street" as an example, here is an intro that I would most likely default to:

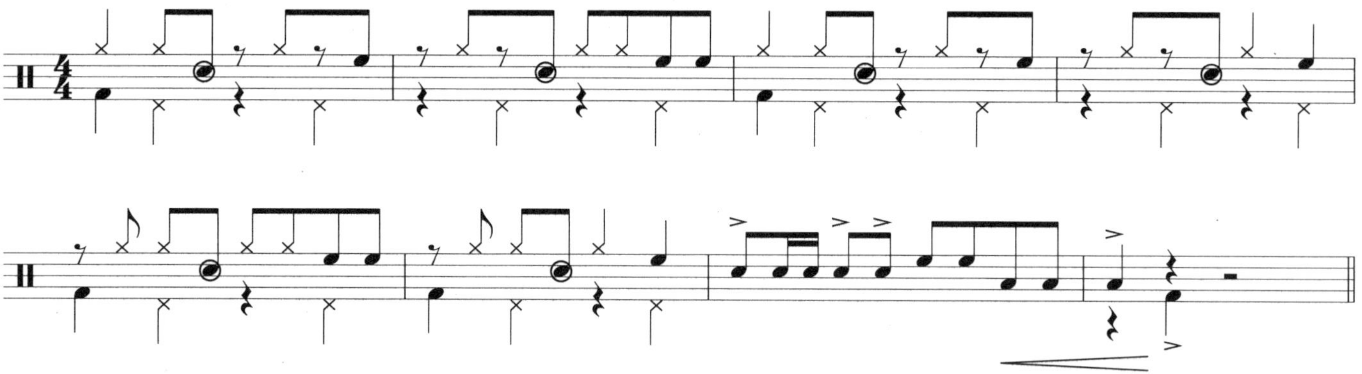

Why do I end it the way I do? To allow the melody to be played in the "open"—that is, in the clear without drums obscuring the entrance or pickup of the melody.

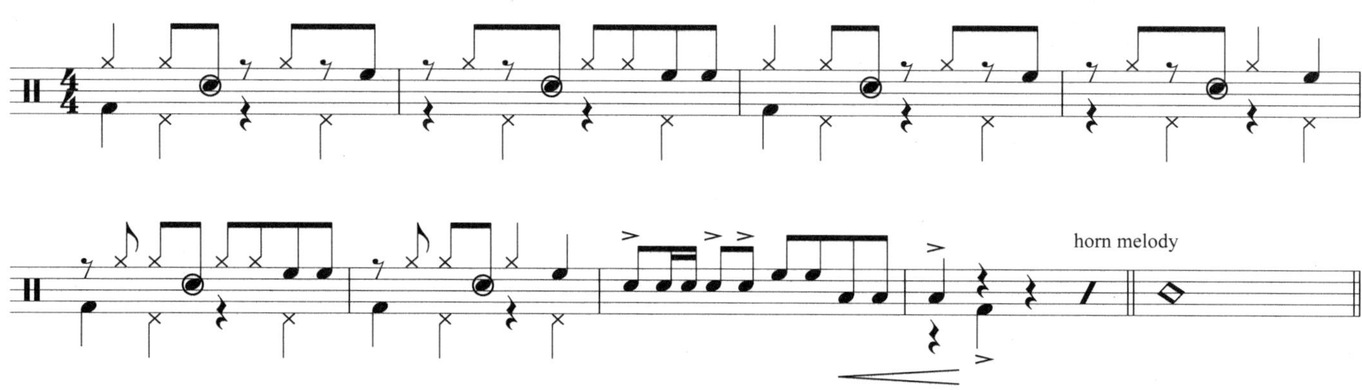

But there's more to this than meets the eye. Actually, meeting the eye is *exactly* what needs to be going on. Eye contact is *essential* to best cue the other musicians when you're about to wrap up so they can make their entrance. Remember: The other players need to prep their embouchures (chops, lips on the horn) or otherwise position their hands and fingers to come in. So we want not only to extend that necessary courtesy, but it's also a good idea to look up and make sure that everyone is inclined and ready to play!

Why would I play that particular intro, by the way? Because "Green Dolphin Street" enjoys a dual feel as far as most jazz interpretations go: "Latin" feel for the first part of the head (eight bars of the melody), followed by eight bars of swing, and so on. ("Latin" is in quotes because that's the expression most commonly used, but "Afro-Cuban" or "Afro-Caribbean" would be more correct. The real world is not a music conservatory, however.) In other words, I'm setting up the feel idiomatically. (There's nothing like the smell of big words in the morning. Name that movie.)

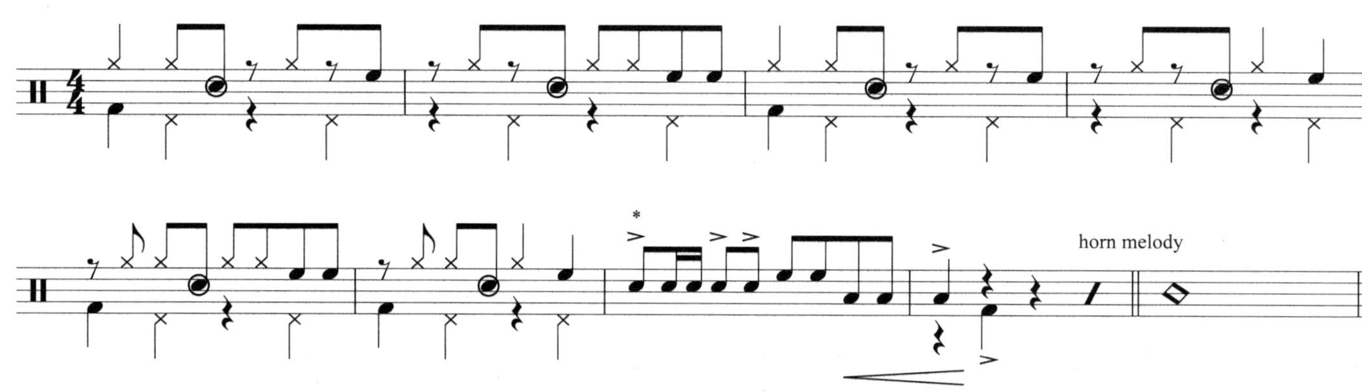

*LOOK UP to other musicians.

That's right. LOOK UP.

Moving on to another example: "Let's play 'St. Thomas.' Hey, drums, take the intro."

Task List:

1. Get the tempo set in your head but don't take three minutes to do so. This should be more like a three-second process at most.
2. Know the beat.
3. PLAY the beat.
4. QUOTE the song.
5. LOOK UP.
6. HAVE FUN.

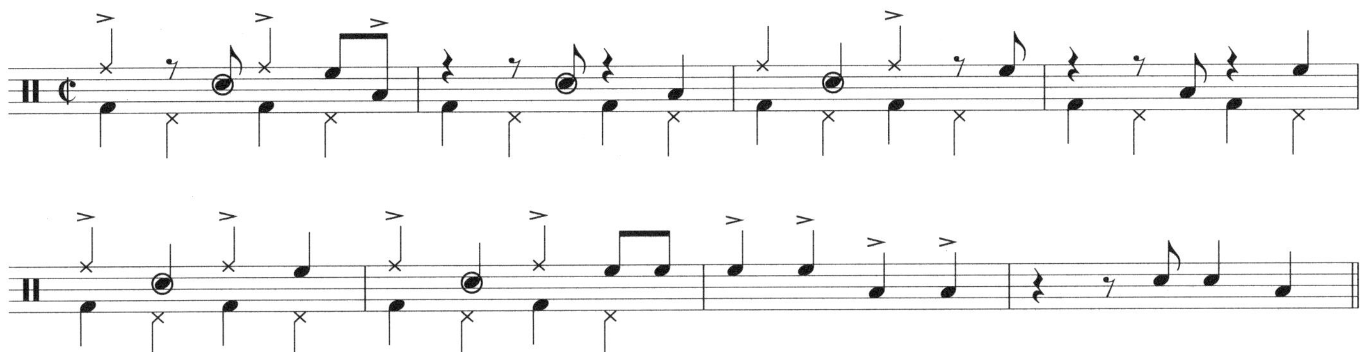

A drum intro is nothing to be scared of. But you'll really be doing yourself a favor if you begin practicing drum intros *now*, because they are a fact of life.

Scene: restaurant gig with a vocalist. She's gotten a request to sing "One Note Samba," and she suggests that you start it.

Fast.

And soft.

With sticks.

What do you do?

Now would be a good time to discuss the *temperature* of the tune, and how the drum intro literally sets the stage for that. Did the singer need to specify "soft"? Not really. You're working (in this hypothetical situation) with a vocalist, so that equals *soft*. The gig is in a restaurant, so that equals *soft*. "One Note Samba," regardless of the tempo, is not a fiery-burn-down-the-house sort of tune, so that equals *soft*.

I would suggest that, instead of applying that samba beat you learned in school to this challenging circumstance, that you use your brain and ears and adhere to the age-old truth that the shortest distance between two points is a straight line. What's the simplest way to play a samba? Or, try that samba beat you learned in Chapter 4 of this book!

For my money, it's all hands on deck, so I'll use both of my hands on the hi-hat with sticks (or brushes on the snare drum) to articulate the essence of the samba beat.

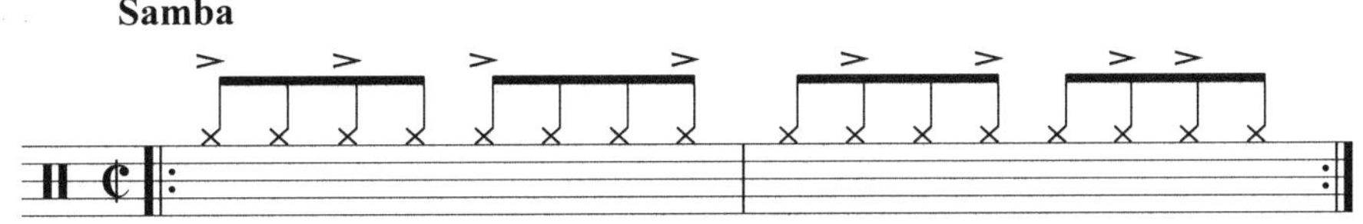

However, even when playing samba, I will often default to playing a bossa nova accent pattern, because it swings and it's fun.

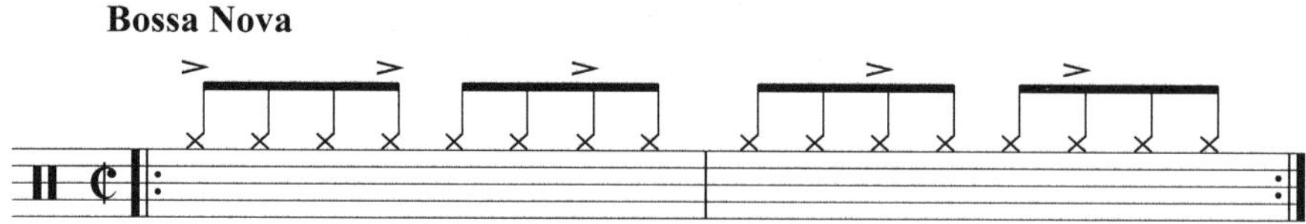

Adding the bass drum, I play the first note of the bar with a dead stroke (letting the beater rest against the head to muffle the stroke) and then bounce the beater off the head for an "open" stroke. This suggests or sounds like the Brazilian *surdo* drum (the second half of the bar is accented). It also manages to keep the beat uncluttered.

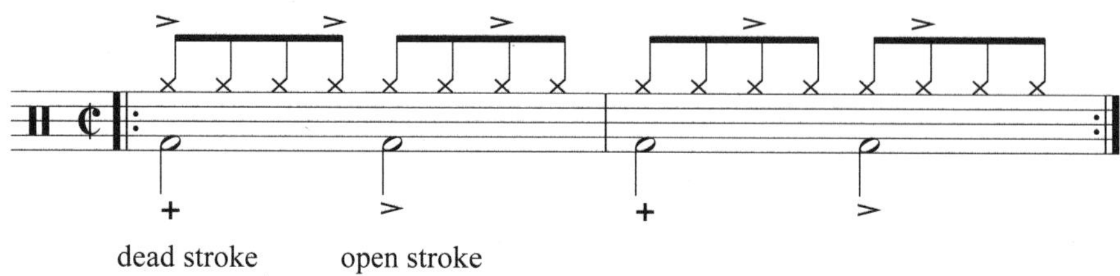

It's *your* intro, so use your ears and decide if you like what you're playing or not. Helpful hint: Use dynamics and strive for simplicity, clarity, and musicality over flash. That said, play what *you'd* like to hear.

And remember: "You do not need to save the world with your drum solo." Besides, an intro is not a solo.

CHAPTER 11

MOTIVIC DEVELOPMENT

> *"The real composer thinks about his work the whole time; he is not always conscious of this, but he is aware of it later when he suddenly knows what he will do."*
>
> —Igor Stravinsky

You can sometimes take the simplest groups of eighth notes and triplets and really develop them into something. To illustrate, I would like to draw from my recording *Motion Poet*, on the Denon label. The first tune on the album is entitled "Erskoman" (composed by me and arranged by Vince Mendoza; the tune is discussed further in Chapter 17). It starts with a calypso-like bass line, played by Will Lee. The bass and drum parts look like this:

The bass drum and cross-stick snare parts are basic and repetitive. They form the body of the groove. The hi-hat, with its syncopation, creates an interesting counter-rhythm and makes an otherwise solid and simple beat dance along. As the melody, which is itself syncopated (and quirky), enters and develops, the hi-hat part becomes more "regular"...

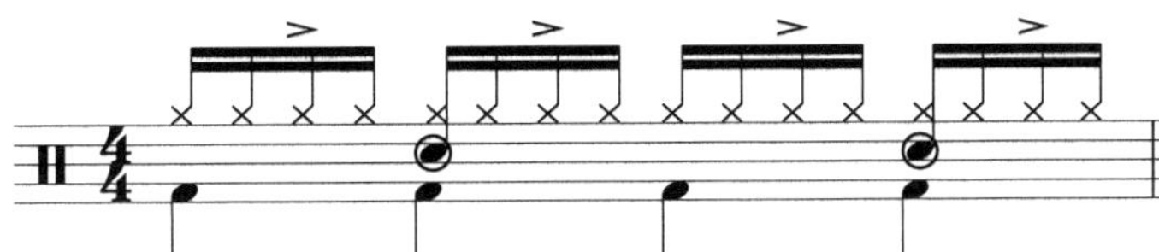

...and simple.

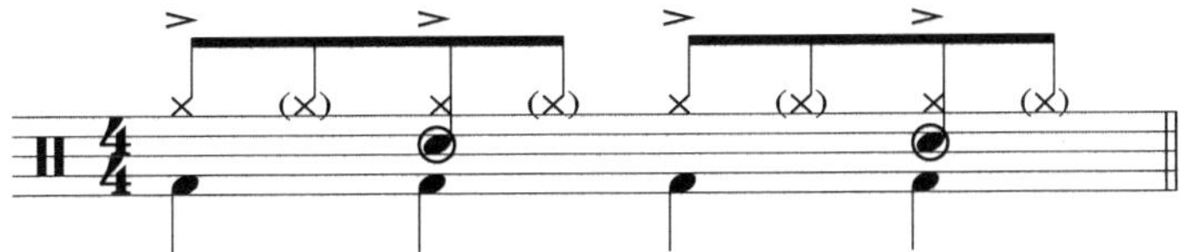

The arrangement produces more and more horn and guitar counter-lines and syncopations, so *by necessity* the drum part stays simple and solid. A groove is great fun to play, and I think that we can agree that by so-called "jazz-fusion" standards, the previous groove is about as basic as we're going to get. This groove has a chance to fly a little bit more when I go from hi-hat to ride cymbal. The hi-hat now plays in a double-time manner, thus giving the music another subtle dimension (i.e., another level of time).

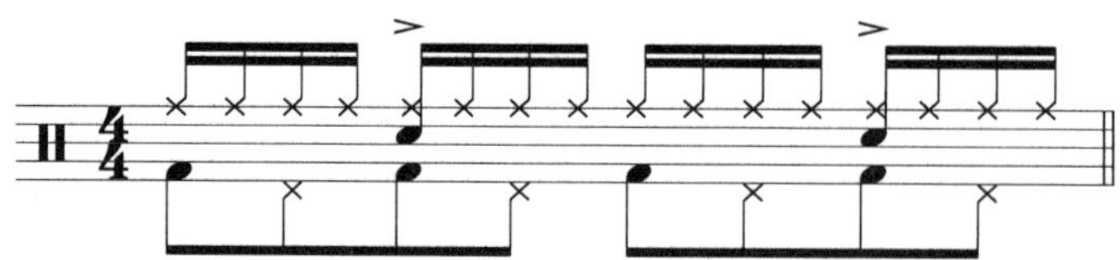

One advantage of the drummer being the composer of a tune is that the composer doesn't need to instruct the drummer as to how the drum part should go! Also, the drum ego is sublimated, in part, by the composition's unfolding and development. Anyway, I get to have some real drum fun for eight bars. A solo! Motivically, I draw from the spirit, as well as the ensemble figures, of the tune.

Although it is a drum solo, you'll notice that there's not a whole lot of ink used in the transcription. As I improvised, I was just trying to compose some more of the tune, then and there—not just play some flashy licks (I don't know too many, anyway) or something else that my hands just "knew." The solo is, I hope, unique, musical, and complementary to the rest of the music. (The entire song can be heard on audio Track 44.)

CHAPTER 12
YOUR RELATIONSHIP TO THE MUSIC AND TO OTHER MUSICIANS

> *"Chamber music—a conversation between friends."*
>
> —Catherine D. Bowen

It's necessary to trust the music in order to be able to transcend it, let alone realize it. A common mistake that many jazz musicians make, I believe, is to initially try to make the music "hipper" than it is, thereby circumventing any chance to really know what is inherently "within" a particular piece of music. That's a very large part of how I have arrived at my style of drumming, which, for better or worse (I believe it's better), is unique.

A lot of the music I play simply involves listening to the other musicians; I can't go in with any preconceived ideas of how it's going to be. For example, one of the first ECM records I played on was *Guamba* by Gary Peacock, who plays bass a little more on top of the beat than I was used to. He also plays around the beat a lot; you don't get a lot of downbeats.

On the first take, I had trouble following him. I wasn't exactly trusting what he was playing. But as I listened to the playback, I could hear exactly what he was doing. The way he was developing around the motion of the music was ingenious. Then, the producer, Manfred Eicher, came over to me and said, "Listen. Just listen."

When we played again, I just listened to Gary without worrying about the beat. The musicians all had enough experience to supply the beat for themselves. So that was one of the first times that I played something where the time wasn't being played, but it was always there. It turned out to be an extraordinary take. I was thrilled.

One aspect of trust involves having confidence in the fact that everyone in the band knows the music well enough so that there is no need to worry about mechanical aspects (e.g., the form of the tune or the technique involved). This frees us to be more "in the moment" and to develop a higher group concentration and interaction, leading to a "whole" concept of music, as opposed to just playing time, heads, and solos.

Communication

I never start off too mysteriously. Even with musicians I know, what I play is always clear until I get a feel for what we're setting up and identify the reference point. With musicians I don't know, I want to make sure they are comfortable with and trust what I'm playing. If I trust myself and am not fighting the music and can play simply and directly, the other musicians will trust me; and if I can trust the other musicians in terms of the consistency and accuracy of their rhythmic placement, then I know I can start moving things around.

When playing with a bass player that you know is locked in, you can engage in some rhythmic displacement. If you're not playing with a strong bass player, he might think the beat got turned around. So that trust relationship is important, and that's why reference points have to be established. You wouldn't start doing that kind of thing right off the bat with musicians you've never worked with. You need to suss out the bass player's placement and security.

Musical experience is very valuable. You should try to play as much as possible with other musicians. And when you do play with other musicians, you need to listen. You can't force too much of your own agenda. Bring your experience and your abilities to the proceedings, but then let the music tell you what to play and respond accordingly.

You'll know better how to do this if you've worked with enough musicians. For example, I've worked with enough bass players that, if it's a 4/4 jazz context and the bass player starts to deviate from the quarter-note pulse and start playing upbeats, I know those upbeats are going to sound great in combination/contrast with the on-the-beat quarter notes that I'm playing. This is because I'm establishing a reference point. I often talk about that in terms of "Mickey Mousing." By staying true to what I'm doing and allowing the other players to do something else, I'm not handcuffing them. If I jump on it every time they try to break away, inexperience would lead me to believe I'm being sensitive. Experience teaches you that most bass players hate that.

I occasionally play with bass players who are otherwise very good, but every time I try to supply some rhythmic counterpoint to the 4/4 groove, they interpret that as, "Oh, cool. We can open it up," and they join me. So I have to go back to straight 4/4, whereas my original idea was to create rhythmic counterpoint.

The first time I played with Miroslav Vitous, he said, "Whenever I started to anticipate or lay back, you kept the time. That was fantastic. Most European drummers follow me when I do that—and I hate that." I know from my experience that when I play with Marc Johnson, if I go in one area, it's nice if he doesn't. If he goes somewhere else, it's nice if I don't. At the same time, we're familiar enough with each other's playing that if, in the middle of a tune, we decide to change the tempo, we don't even have to look at each other. We just hear each other and change the tempo. So experience is necessary for musicians to be aware of the possibilities.

I should hasten to add that I'm not suggesting that it's always OK to change a tempo in the middle of a song. Marc and I used to do that with John Abercrombie's trio, and the group verbally and otherwise was committed to doing that kind of thing. But I could only be comfortable doing that because two weeks earlier I had done a breakfast cereal commercial in which I didn't have four or eight measures to get into the groove. Right from the downbeat, it's twenty-eight seconds of music that has to be right on the money. That kind of discipline and that ability to focus pays off in spades when you're improvising and playing "free form" music because your performance or note placement, whether it's free or not, is very specific.

I played with a bass player once who was trying to do all this thumb popping stuff during a tune, and it just wasn't happening. On the break, he was practicing all that stuff as fast as he could play it, and that was the problem. He never practiced it in the real tempo of the song. If you just practice flash and speed, where does that get you in the middle of a tune?

In terms of not Mickey Mousing someone else, I'm reminded of when Weather Report toured the USA (autumn of 1978) and recorded four shows, resulting in the *8:30* album. During Joe Zawinul's "Black Market," Wayne Shorter and I improvised a "duet." An interesting lesson that I learned from the recording of that particular performance was not to confuse complementary music-making with copy-cat music-making. In other words, in that duet, I sometimes tended to imitate Wayne rhythmically (hemiolas, etc.), instead of providing a base, or counterpoint, to the conversation. At the time, I thought that I had "big ears," but when I listen to it now, it's a little bit more like I had a big mouth. When accompanying a soloist, that soloist will be counting on you to keep a point of reference for him or her to play off of. Jumping onto their bandwagon can destroy that beautiful tension and release that they are attempting to accomplish.

Oftentimes, fellow musicians or bandleaders have difficulty conveying what it is they want or need from the drums. For example, when I was in Weather Report, Zawinul would often look over at the drums and gesture for "more!" Sometimes I would respond by playing louder; other times I would play busier. And still, he would yell for "more!" But I thought I was giving him "more!"

Nowadays, if someone asks me for "more," I'll usually interpret that to mean an increase in the music's intensity, which can be accomplished by a combination of means, usually involving dynamics, density, and emotionally evocative drumming choices (involving the use of rhythm and orchestration on the kit). "More" doesn't necessarily equate to playing faster or louder alone. I can achieve "more" by playing fewer notes all of a sudden, where each accent begins to stand out and shine amidst the building intensity of the tune, really adding to the emotional crescendo. In that case, we can apply the classic advice: "Less is more."

"More" can also mean playing the time with added intensity and concentration. "More" might mean "more in the style of" a particular band's music. (I can imagine a school band director asking for "more" in the case of playing a Basie chart and needing it to really swing hard.) So the word begs for "more" than simply playing louder or faster.

Sometimes, it's a good idea to try to verbalize such musical concerns away from the bandstand. I've always found that reasonable discussion (i.e., without defensiveness or insult) can solve a musical problem, providing that some talent, experience, and willingness are present. (Record producers often speak their own language in these circumstances!) It's the responsibility of all musicians to try their best to make the music sound its best, and that includes being able to effectively communicate one's wishes.

Ego

It's natural to be self-conscious when playing in front of others, whether an audience, your peers, or both. The focus becomes all the more critical when various distractions tug at the performer. It's all a matter of doing it enough so that you get more and more comfortable playing in concert. There is also the factor that, when you're playing live, you're generally playing with other musicians as opposed to self-absorbed practicing by yourself, where musical context can easily be forgotten.

The clear rendering of a simple idea can be much more difficult than it seems. You can become a victim of your own or other people's built-up expectations of virtuosity. I've seen that with a lot of musicians. People felt that they didn't get their money's worth unless a particular musician did that over-the-top thing that, at some point, was very exciting to people. With certain drummers, people won't leave them alone until they do some spectacular kind of thing, but maybe the music isn't asking for that.

I get angry with myself if I do things technically that the music doesn't call for, just to live up to some kind of "yahoo" expectation. I've pretty much given that up. Within the context of what I do, I can still pull out some stuff and play exciting and with passion. I can hit the drums with enough power and authority plus dexterity and speed to not only fulfill the musical objective but to be entertaining—if the music or the moment calls for that.

Part of the pleasure of playing an instrument can be found in those flights of fancy. Let the soloist show off in those great concertos. Sometimes when you play, if you are just trying to serve the music through timekeeping, the other elements in the band might be such that not a whole lot is happening. So it might be your responsibility to create some excitement or interest. But it has to all be within the service of the music.

All of that being said, however, it does bear pointing out that the clear rendering of a simple idea can be much harder than it seems. When the music is relatively uncomplicated, everything you play is very exposed sonically, and so touch and tone become especially important. The pay-off is that you are expressing a musical idea as opposed to entertaining someone's built-up expectations of virtuosity. True virtuosity lies in the ability to deliver either a simple musical idea or some very difficult/sophisticated harmonic and rhythmic material with an effortless flow, so that the technique involved doesn't call attention to itself.

Playing with Intention

The job of the drummer is to provide rhythmic information to the band and the listener. How we do that is a matter of choice. Sometimes, that choice is dictated by the stylistic demands of the music; other times it's an intuitive response to what you hear from the musicians you are working with. A musician who spends enough time playing time is then able to play with the time in such a way that forward motion can be clearly felt (even though you're not playing, for example, a steady quarter-note pulse), because each note you play is informed by that experience. If you're just imitating free playing without understanding it contrapuntally—which is how I used to play free—then the foundation isn't there. It doesn't take much of a breeze to come along and blow the house down, as it were.

So playing with intention became the thing that I needed to learn, and that became the guiding principle of what I called "anti-drumming." I was inspired by a film documentary called *Shadows and Light*, which is about directors of photography. At one point, they interview the director of photography for the film *Rosemary's Baby*. He describes a scene with a view down a hallway into a bedroom, and Mia Farrow is sitting on the bed talking on the phone. The director, Roman Polanski, told him, "I only want to see the back of her head with the phone on her ear; don't show the front half of her face." During the premiere, that scene came on, and they saw everyone in the audience lean their heads to try to look around the corner to see her face.

To put that in more concrete musical terms, in James Brown's "Mother Popcorn," there is an open beat on beat 4, and you can't help but shake your booty to fill that vacuum. Nature abhors a vacuum, right? So the genius of James Brown, or of filmmakers or poets, is leaving things unsaid. What you don't play makes it an interactive listening experience for the other musicians and your audience.

That became kind of the cornerstone of my "anti-drumming" thing. It wasn't really "anti" drumming, but I was trying to figure out how to create those same kinds of moments by not being so implicit to where there is no role for the listener's imagination. If I do that with a firm grasp of the subdivisions, that stuff is all implied. If things get too explicit, the music loses a lot of charm. That's why I think space is a dynamic and interesting thing. But you have to respect it and not treat space like it's something to rush through as quickly as possible.

I don't know how concerned a lot of fast drumming is with space. And of course, when you think of fast drumming, you think of Buddy Rich. What does everyone still talk about as being his most incredible break? It's the one on "Love for Sale," when he plays this startling single-stroke roll on the snare and STOPS. And then, the band comes in. It's thrilling. You've just been taken to the edge of the abyss. You hear the audience react in delight. He took everyone's breath away for a second.

So that's that kind of thing that fascinated me. But when you play the drums, people want to hear you *play the drums*. I explored the "anti-drumming" thing as far as I could figure out how to take it, and I was even beginning to regard myself as less of a drummer. I would listen to Tony Williams or Jack DeJohnette and find myself thinking, "There's a drummer. I'm an accompanist." I wouldn't even dare put myself in the same category as "drummer" with those guys. But now I'm feeling more and more like a drummer.

As Manfred Eicher told me many years ago: "Listen. Just listen."

CHAPTER 13
PUTTING IDEAS INTO ACTION

My dear old friend, the late John Abercrombie, used to say when drinking his favorite breakfast beverage, "You know, there's nothing like a good cup of coffee in the morning... and this is *nothing* like a good cup of coffee." Ha! But, humor aside, there is nothing like a good recording session to get your hands, feet, heart, and mind all on the same page. Such was the case when I traveled from Los Angeles to New York City to go into the studio with stalwarts John Scofield on guitar, Uri Caine on piano, and Scott Colley on bass. The purpose of accompanying flugelhorn artist Franco Ambrosetti on his new album, with string arrangements by Alan Broadbent, was the reason for my trip. We had two days to record eight tunes, and we managed to get six of the songs finished by the end of day one. *This* was a good recording session.

The strings were added onto the tracks on days three and four, so we had Sibelius/Note Performer renderings of string parts (actually quite realistic and helpful to hear) that were married to an annoying metronome sound (unrealistic and not-so-helpful, but there it was). How to best deal with this on a practical as well as on a musical level? Oh yeah, did I mention that I was playing on the studio's "house" kit? How shall I put this? They sang in a far different key from my drums at home.

It's All About Making Adjustments

The first thing I did was to make sure that my mindset was in "eager acceptance" mode of the kit. I treated the drums with joy. Does that sound too "new age"? All I can say is: Try it. And once peace has been made with the drums (as well as all squeaks and offensive sounds being vetted out of the room), I panned the clicks to the right side of my headset, so as to allow for me to position the left headphone cup away from my ear in order to hear the drums acoustically in the room. It's always helpful to hear the actual sound of the instrument when playing (and the panning trick is to prevent any click sounds from escaping the unworn earcup).

While treating the drums with joy, I treat the music and musicians with joy as well, even though I am deadly serious when it comes to the actual playing. Wait... balancing *joy* with being as *serious* as a heart attack? *This is the balance of creation.* And so... even though I have been part of, literally, thousands of recording sessions over the years, I discovered something quite new on this date. I'll term it as follows:

The creation of, or allowing of, more horizontal freedom and width.

Wha-a-a?

The creation of, or allowing of, more horizontal freedom and width prevents the playing of the "same old, same old" over and over again.

Huh?

OK. All of this came about during the tracking of Miles Davis's "All Blues," which has a bit of an open/repeating vamp now and then, but is otherwise married to form. So the form is there, and the song is pretty well-known by most musicians as well as jazz listeners. "All Blues" does not need the drums to emphasize the downbeat at the top of each chorus. Nor does it need the usual delineation of phrases within the choruses (playing fills and constructing comping devices) to build to the "usual suspects" of rhythmic destination points—either the downbeat or the "and" of beat 4.

What does that mean?

With the always-excellent, but unusually-excellent-on-this-particular-afternoon Scott Colley on bass, I felt free to concentrate on my own compositional motifs in the form of triplets or combinations of twos and threes (remember those?). I was joy-filled to either play "consonant" rhythms or "dissonant" rhythms that crossed the grain of the time flow. And I was NOT resolving those tensions where drummers usually resolve them.

For example:

Did it work?

All I can tell you is that, during the playback in the control room, Scott quickly walked across the room to pinch the skin between my shoulder and neck in a sort of "*atta boy*" gesture of appreciation and mutual admiration. And he was smiling.

I was exploring playing over the barline, and through the endings and beginnings of phrases. I did this by creating specific statements that went beyond the point of natural resolution during the tune, and I plan to continue doing so from here on out.

These were not flourishes or flashy runs. Everything I played was clear, clean, simple, motivic, and repeated to the point of making each of these ideas memorable and, dare I say, meaningful!

I'll put it this way: Once you begin to compose at the drumset, all sorts of doors and windows will open for you. And (dig this), not just for you, but ALL of the musicians will sense the broadening of, and the addition of, *width* to the music. It's a bit like magic. Even the pre-recorded string track seemed to respond positively.

In teaching this idea to my university students, I stated all of the above. But then I added this wrinkle while each of them played: "Hey, your cymbals and toms all just disappeared. Play time on the snare drum." Their first instinct was to play *soloistically* on the snare, or to begin moving their arms and wrists in an odd, exaggerated manner (that betrayed their being ill-at-ease and overthinking the problem).

The Shortest Distance Between Two Points?

Right: A straight line. Yet, no matter how creative we feel impelled, compelled, or required to be, isn't our primary job to provide rhythmic information? So hey, how about some quarter notes on the snare drum? Play them just like you'd play quarter notes on a ride cymbal, only softer! So now, we can deal with how to make *that* swing. It will because it must. And then, the magic happens.

The sonics have opened up the music, and our musical choices have opened up the music. Our compositional skills are getting stronger by the second because we are giving ourselves the permission to make music as opposed to play the drums and play some *hip stuff*. We are ignoring the desire to *play like so-and-so* because of who-knows-what reason; we're always torturing ourselves in this way.

> *Give yourself permission to play simply and to play with joy (all the while being as serious as a heart attack).*

Find a good play-along track or app or get together with your rhythm section/bandmates to explore playing over the barline. (Raise your hand if you know who Kenny Clarke was.) How does *intention* and *specificity* fit into this?

CHAPTER 14

FREE PLAYING

> *"Each thing you hear determines the direction that you go. You just follow the music, and if you follow the music you can go anywhere."*
>
> —Steve Lacy, from *The Man with the Straight Horn*, quoted by Richard Scott

Writing about music, it has been said, is as effective as dancing about architecture. It is especially thorny to try to demonstrate musical concepts about "free" or "open" styles of drumming, while only having access to a word processor. A few years ago, while I was writing a series of columns for *Modern Drummer* magazine, my trusted editor, Rick Mattingly, recommended that I describe and display an open style of jazz drumming, "something in between chaos and hitting a strong downbeat in every bar." Hmmm. Food for thought.

Before sitting down behind the computer, I set pencil to paper, and came up with these two thoughts:

LISTENING TO OTHER MUSICIANS

§

MAKING YOUR OWN STATEMENT

Next, I drew this symbol:

And then I turned on the television.

While the Public Broadcasting System news was recapping the day's events, I stared at my piece of paper and considered my incomplete thesis. Playing "free" isn't exactly "listening to other musicians" as opposed to "making your own statement"; rather, it is a more "hand-in-glove" type of concept, so that my drawing of the Tao, or the yin-yang symbol, seemed to graphically make good sense. The musician has to be acutely aware of everything else that the other musicians are playing, yet must be able to make his or her own unique musical statement, without being merely imitative.

I then wrote down the notion that "everything is timekeeping." This stems from my belief that any and all colors, sounds, or rhythms that I play on the drums function as timekeeping. Not only do they bear witness to the velocity taking place, they are the heartbeat, pulse, and frame of reference for all forward movement in the music. In more basic terms, I don't approach drumming as, "I'll play three bars of time, now I'll play a fill, and now I'll play some time again..." Everything is timekeeping, whether or not it's played on the ride cymbal.

Next to that idea, I drew an arrow with the added thought that, "Music is not just notes."

Before I had the chance to scribble any more profundities onto paper, the PBS show *Nova* came on the air. I decided to watch, and a remarkable coincidence took place. The topic of *Nova* that evening was "The Order of Chaos." The same word that Rick had used to orientate my thinking for describing "free" drumming—chaos—was what this show was about! So I watched, and I kept my pad of paper handy for taking notes.

The next day, while browsing in an airport bookstore, I happened upon a copy of *Chaos: Making a New Science*, by James Gleick. Another coincidence!

Chaos science is mathematical in origin but is manifested in everyday life. The study of chaos reveals patterns, and a hidden order in nature and cyclic events. It has brought together many disciplines of science (mathematics, physics, biology, etc.). As you'll see, we may have fun with language and include drumming and free music, too.

As Gleick explains in his book:

> The first chaos theorists... shared certain sensibilities. They had an eye for pattern, especially pattern that appeared on different scales at the same time. They had a taste for randomness and complexity, for jagged edges and sudden leaps. Believers in chaos... speculate about determinism and free will, about evolution, about the nature of conscious intelligence... they are looking for the whole.

Sounds like a job description for a free-jazz musician!

Predictability is a very important part of traditional science (as well as pop and mainstream music). But we can discover more about those things around us if we will consider that seemingly random behavior does have its own order—some sort of structure or containment. A relatively simple mathematical equation can model a turbulent or violent phenomenon. The more open-ended result comes from the fact that tiny differences in input can quickly become overwhelming differences in output—a factor given the name "sensitive dependence on initial conditions." In other words, a chain of events can reach a point of crisis where small changes are magnified dramatically. Chaos would have us understand that such points are everywhere; i.e., they are pervasive.

In 1961, while attempting to produce complex behavior in a computer model, a scientist named Edward Lorenz came up with a system of just three equations. Gleick elaborates:

> They were nonlinear, meaning that they expressed relationships that were not strictly proportional. Linear relationships can be captured with a straight line on a graph. Linear relationships are easy to think about: The more the merrier. Linear equations are solvable, which makes them suitable for textbooks. Linear systems have an important modular virtue: You can take them apart and put them together again—the pieces add up.
>
> Nonlinear systems generally cannot be solved and cannot be added together. In fluid systems and mechanical systems, the nonlinear terms tend to be the features that people want to leave out when they try to get a good, simple understanding. Friction, for example. Without friction, a simple linear equation expresses the amount of energy you need to accelerate a hockey puck.
>
> With friction the relationship gets complicated, because the amount of energy changes depending on how fast the puck is already moving. Nonlinearity means that the act of playing the game has a way of changing the rules. You cannot assign a constant importance to friction because its importance depends on speed. Speed, in turn, depends on friction. That twisted changeability makes nonlinearity hard to calculate, but it also creates rich kinds of behavior that never occur in linear systems.

You may have guessed that the ubiquitous appearance of the words "linear" and "nonlinear" in discussions of chaos further intrigued and excited me. The so-called "linear" style of drumming represents, to me anyway, a rather calculated and controlled method of timekeeping and beat-making—relatively easy to present by way of transcription, tidy in execution, neat, and not very messy.

Nonlinear drumming is, for me, a potentially much more expressive form and approach to music-making. The flow, torrent, and calm of such drummers' music as Ed Blackwell, Paul Motian, Jack DeJohnette, Andrew Cyrille, Roy Haynes, Rashied Ali, Ra Kalem Bob Moses, Elvin Jones, et al, is rich in sound, color, and motion, and not very easy to notate on paper. Indeed, I would suggest that the student who listens to them for the purpose of transcribing their drumming may well be missing the point. Remember, we want to be able to see the forest as well as the trees. Our time is much better spent listening to the music—letting it enrich our lives—and then intuitively attempting to achieve the velocity, flow, or calm of these drumming masters' performances. I suggest listening to the music of such musicians as Ornette Coleman, Keith Jarrett, and Paul Bley.

When I listen to "Ghosts" (Albert Ayler and Milford Graves), the pulse is so strong even if it has the appearance or semblance of being free. Milford couldn't have been a timbalero in New York without having had an unbelievable sense of time. When someone has such an innately strong sense of time no matter what they play, it's present. The time is always there.

I don't mean this to be an indictment of "linear" drumming studies (not too much, anyway). But all of this says to me: Trust your ears, mind, and heart to play this, or any other kind of music. Listen to everything that the other musicians are playing and respond appropriately, as your taste and experience can determine. Summon up patience and courage. Experiment. Discover the hidden architecture in spontaneously composed music. And, if this has shed any light at all on how I approach listening to and playing free music, then I encourage you to broaden your scope of studies, too. There's a lot to be learned about drumming from life.

Free music doesn't imply just flurries of notes or getting in touch with the angst of your soul or whatever. By carefully listening and suggesting at different points along the way where the music can go, then it's truly free. Patience is crucial.

In free playing, we tend to get more involved with the instrument texturally. We do things that might not otherwise be proper, such as laying the stick across the cymbal more, or playing parts of the kit that we might not otherwise play, like the shells of the drums, shaking a stick between two rack toms. Such sounds often work in an improvisational structure.

Leonard Bernstein made an interesting point about atonal music, such as 12-tone or serial compositional technique. It's not atonal. All of those tones have tone, and any combination of notes fulfill or suggest some harmonic function. So likewise, rhythmically, you can do any number of rhythmic juxtapositions and they can be right. Some note combinations sound better than others. Some lead your mind's ear to one place, and a skilled composer will take it somewhere where it's a revelation. They can even take the listener somewhere obvious, whereas an unskilled composer will take it someplace where the momentum has stopped. I've often used the analogy of walking and then having both feet land at the same time as you step off the curb. The flow stops.

So flow is determined not only by touch on the instrument but the intellectual choice of what we play and where we play it. But anything is possible.

I was in David Baker's band at Indiana University. David was always saying "Free it up, free it up." We were doing this free thing, and my teacher, George Gaber, poked his head in the door. I was thinking, "This stuff is so modern I don't know if he'll dig what we're doing." He waited until our next lesson and said, "I heard you playing the other night. It sounded like the three of you weren't listening to one another—but other than that, what I heard sounded good." I headed back to the drawing board.

Years later, I was working in the recording studio with East-German born pianist Joachim Kühn. Two of Joachim's favorite words in English are the adjectives "burning" and "free." Perhaps you can guess what the music was like. I recount these words being used in more of a qualitative than quantitative sense.

Anyway, the directions he gave the band were simply this: "Let's not talk about it," and, "Playing free will make you happy." (I had been grumbling as to when we were going to break for lunch.) Oftentimes, the impression that most people have about free music is that it is a jumbled mass of notes and events. However, as the tape started to roll, this particular performance began to unfold delicately; the music was transparent, pleasant to listen to, and creative. We made a good take (and then I got to eat lunch).

I would like to go over a few of the aesthetic possibilities that we may encounter and enjoy when playing free, or open styles of music.

Space, patience, and balance have become some of the most important words in my musical vocabulary. These words represent, to me, the elements of mature music-making.

- *Space* means to leave breathing room for your own and the other musicians' notes. This will involve the use of rests. In much of the music that I really enjoy playing and listening to, the rests are the best notes (not) played!
- *Patience* goes hand-in-hand with rests, as well as being an essential ingredient of the development of any piece of music. Sometimes it is best (and crucial) to bide your time and make your musical statements at their proper time.
- *Balance* ensures that the notes, rests, ideas, and relative dynamics of the different instruments speak in true accord.

Other components of this music may include the use of colors or textural shadings on the various parts of the drumset. A good example of this would be the use of brushes to "imply" the time—when the forward velocity of the music is determined by the ebb and flow (i.e., the motion) of the brush strokes. The pulse here is neither regular nor obvious. Textures and colors can also be provided by flurries and clusters of notes. Velocity, hence forward motion, is easily sensed here. Another device is to change the tempo at will, speeding up and slowing down the quarter-note pulse (at whim) to achieve the desired effect.

What is the desired effect? To make a highly personal musical statement, and to be modern! One of the purposes of art is to make people look at something familiar in a new light. Developments in both jazz and classical musics have made this provocatively possible. In classical music, the musical possibilities were opened up by the creation of *aleatory music*. The *Harvard Dictionary of Music* defines this as:

> Music in which the composer introduces elements of chance or unpredictability with regard to either the composition or its performance... Chance may be involved in the process of composition, in performance, or both. In the composition process, pitches, durations, degrees of intensity, etc., and/or their distribution in time may be chosen by dice throwing, interpretations of abstract designs (Cage), etc., or according to certain mathematical laws of chance (Xenakis). In performance, chance is allowed to operate by leaving some elements and/or their order of appearance to the performer's discretion (Boulez, Stockhausen, et al), thus introducing the idea of choice. Most of these procedures are derived from and motivated by new general concepts of music, according to which form and structure are no longer regarded as definitely fixed and final but as subject to partial or total transformations from one performance to another (open forms, mobile forms). The composers adhering to such ideas are part of a general movement—in science and philosophy as well as in the arts—that tends to consider, and therefore to express, the world in terms of possibility rather than necessity.

I quote this definition excerpt at length, because: 1) I like it, and; 2) It makes me smile to think that jazz has known this all along. Anyway, the aesthetics and sounds from classical free, or aleatory, music have most certainly found their way into modern jazz expression.

In the context of the performance (or recording) of a piece of free music, I think it is a good idea to remember that tension and release are key factors in a music's success. Tension and release can be expressed as a V7 chord resolving to I, or as a kinetic (and possibly frenetic?) piece of creativity resolving to a purer, cleaner, triumphantly clear passage—expressed tonally, harmonically, and/or rhythmically. Balance is key.

With freedom comes responsibility and a need for discipline. There also comes the opportunity for a full range of expression. (I wonder, though, if it is OK for someone to do the musical equivalent of yelling "FIRE!" in a crowded movie theater?) Anyway, back to that recording session in Germany... More and more, I find myself in playing situations where the musicians will not discuss what it is that's about to be played. No particular song will be in mind; tempos or keys are not talked about or considered. The muse (inspiration/creation/God) strikes, and if the ego is not in the way, the music will start to flow. Creativity and ideas are sparked in the other players.

What can happen? It's like several people meeting all at once and starting a discussion, where no agenda or outline has been prepared or must be observed. In the ideal state, it's not the musicians' fingers that are doing the talking; it's every player's combined wealth of listening, longing, happiness, sadness, knowledge, technique (i.e., language), love, and a playful sense of being alive. I believe it's the musicians' souls that are directly communicating with each other. When we play music, what we are really playing is everything that we've ever been and everything that we hope to be.

Novelist John Cheever once said: "Art is the triumph over chaos." What can we learn from "chaos?"

Johann Wolfgang Goethe wrote: "I have found among my papers a sheet... in which I call architecture frozen music."

Both of these great thinkers recognize that an inherent sense of structure is vital to any art. To simplify matters, though, let's consider again the following advice from Johann Sebastian Bach: "There is nothing to it. You only have to hit the right note at the right time, and the instrument plays itself."

But how do you know where to hit which note at what time?

"What makes good judgment? Experience. What makes experience? Bad judgment."[7]

Go for it!

One of my favorite performances is also one of my more recent, and this comes from an album titled *Live in Italy*, recorded in concert on November 19, 2021, in the town of Camogli (outside of Genoa). It's amazing what good pasta and good acoustics can inspire! The title of the tune, "Three Quarter Molly," is in reference and deference to Elvin Jones' "Three Card Molly," but the tune is very different in tone and meter; I penned it during the great lockdown.

During the drum solo section, which you can hear on audio Track 36, the piano and bass repeat a four-chord vamp while I solo freely atop the time, tempo, and phrases of the song. I opted to eschew or avoid most of the downbeats or resolution (destination) points suggested by the form of the vamp, all the while being completely aware of where the time was. And notice here, in contrast to something discussed previously, the absence of destination points. I felt that this brought my drumming closer than ever before to that of my drumming heroes. If you like this and want to get "here," my suggestion is that you practice the destination-points concept a lot in order to build up your inner time muscle and music awareness radar.

36

7 Guglielmo Ferrero, 19th-century Italian psychologist.

CHAPTER 15
WHERE'S THE ETHOS?

> *"I despise a world which does not feel that music is a higher revelation than all wisdom and philosophy."*
>
> —Ludwig van Beethoven

ethos (noun) [Gr. ethos, disposition, character: see ETHICAL] the characteristic and distinguishing attitudes, habits, beliefs, etc. of an individual or of a group.

When listening to music, whether of my own making or someone else's, I find myself looking, more and more, for those distinguishing moments and features that describe that music (and musician) as coming from some particular place. That language of the musician—music—conveys each musician's own history. Or does it?

Every person has a story to tell. Some stories are more interesting than others, and some people may have a better delivery, but if the effort is made, then at least the musician has attempted to communicate to his or her fellow beings. I can't help but feel, however, that many of us don't take advantage of the opportunity to really say something on our instrument. In other words, we might mark the passing of time with, well, just time.

After all my emphasis on the virtues and necessity of good, solid, simple timekeeping, then what am I talking about now, and why?

Good basic timekeeping is important, and it is certainly the best place to start when drumming. But there can be so much more to it than just that. By so much more, do I mean that the drummer necessarily play any more in a given piece? No. I would hope, though, that the drummer will attempt to put every bit of his or her energy, concentration, taste, and effort into the music—every time.

Talking about this once with pianist and good friend, the late Don Grolnick (a musician whose taste, restraint, and common sense I implicitly admired and trusted), he shared with me a tenet that he had set forth in a lecture given to students at the University of North Texas while he was guest-lecturing there. Not assuming a judgmental point of view, Don chose to offer the students of music (as we all are) the concept of "competing thrills."

There are many different types of thrills that music can bring to us. Perhaps the most powerful one is when we are young and first thrilled by music—that incredible, magical moment when we realize that this is something that will have to be part of our lives forever. Another thrill is when we first pick up the instrument (or, in the drummer's case, a pair of drumsticks) and begin to play. There is the thrill of acceptance (or of being noticed by the opposite sex). And, while learning our instrument, there are more thrills each step of the way, like transcribing someone's solo and getting it right, or coming up with our very own first lick.

As we start playing more and more in public, there is the thrill when something we've done gets a good audience reaction or response. That particular thrill can be in competition with another thrill that can be obtained by playing what the music begged for—answering the highest call of music, in other words.

Music being a creative art form, this is not such a simple task, however. In order to have those moments in which you feel that you have really played the music, you must be open to the possibility of making mistakes. Little ones. Big ones. But those mistakes are noble ones, if made in the pursuit of exploration of your art.

A musician who is a good example of this pursuit is saxophonist Wayne Shorter. Watching Wayne play, Don and I were both struck by how he seemed to really be within the present—looking within and exploring, laying himself open to what occurs to him. Wayne's improvisations may have breathtaking moments, as well as moments where things are not so impressive. The overriding impression, however, is of Wayne's patience, maturity, and excellence. In other words, each solo is not a virtuoso display; rather, it can be an exploration of a particular thing. Wayne takes a thematic idea and develops it. To me, he is like a dancer when he plays.

In a treatise such as this, I must ask the question and then analyze the result. I am not so sure that, for many musicians, this is necessarily such a conscious process. I would suggest that you occasionally think about it, though.

Another quality of this intense, personal involvement with music that I've seen Wayne exhibit is the single-minded pursuit of that musically thrilling moment, or event, without the awareness of the audience or its reaction. Contrary to some other musicians (too many now, I'm afraid), who are playing to their audience, fully conscious and expectant of the audience's reaction, players who follow their musical heart fulfill, I believe, the calling that music made so deeply to them when they were young.

So the main "competing thrill" that Don Grolnick talked about is this: Don discovered that he had a few licks in his repertoire that could be done impressively. There was always a positive listener response. But he opted for the "higher road," trying to focus his skills and choices towards the more musical end. After a while, Don couldn't even appreciate that lesser thrill of the audience's applause for those few licks when he did play them. Subsequently, he started to remove those elements and devices from his playing.

I think about these things. The opportunities to be musical are always there; it's just a matter of training oneself to see (and hear) them—taking the time to smell the roses. Musical discipline and aesthetic pursuit. It's a rewarding way to play the drums. And ultimately, it is a revealing way to play. Because then, I think that it is impossible to approach your music as a "product." Rather, it is a highly personal art—one which, when you are honest with yourself, cannot be thought of (certainly not first) in commercial terms. A refreshing thought in these times, no?

Here's another viewpoint, courtesy of a gentleman named A.K. Coomaraswamy. He was an art historian and curator at the Boston Museum of Fine Arts from 1917 to the early '40s, whose writings have been influential in the art world. As opposed to the concept of the artist seeking to realize the maximum of self-expression (and, by the way, ego), he felt the following way: "The free man is not trying to express himself, but that which (is) to be expressed... it is never Who said? but only What was said? that concerns us." There are obviously good examples of this sentiment to be found in Zen and anonymous religious art.

This presents us with a triangle of aesthetic choices and guidelines:

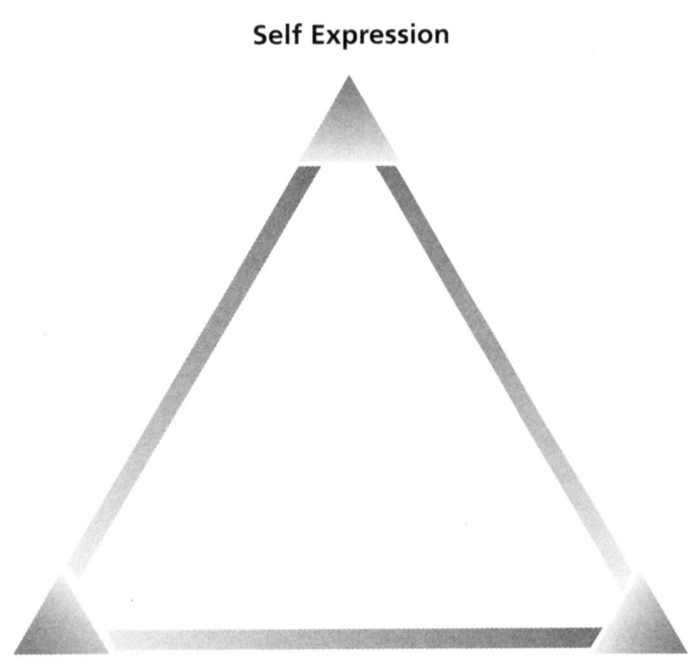

I know which sides of the triangle I'd like to lean toward. How about you?

Finally, allow me to present a quote made by another gentleman from the art world for you to put in your pipe and smoke as you please...

"It took me four years to paint like Raphael, but a lifetime to paint like a child." —Pablo Picasso

CHAPTER 16

TEN SECRETS OF THE DRUMMING LIFE

When writing or speaking about drumming and music, there always seems to be the very real risk of stating the obvious. Though many enduring truths are really quite simple, they seem to be those types of things that require the occasional reminder or pointing out. If you're feeling at all in awe of another's drumming and are wondering what might be missing from your musical cupboard, let's revisit some "Tried and True Tenets of the Traps." Many of the following points come up regularly in my discussions with music students.

1. **Music should be fun.** You don't need to smile when you're playing, but it helps when and if you do. Even if that smile is on the inside, the realization and expression of gratitude for being able to be part of the music-making miracle helps tremendously to open one's mind, spirit, and heart. This means that the ears open up all the more; hearing is really about receptivity. When all seems "right" with the world, I find that my muscles relax, and my entire sense of being glows in the music-making process. And, while playing music, I can make most everything seem "right" with the world because art is the refuge of the imagination. It's about finding the joy in the things that you do. One night I was working on a Burger King jingle; I had a ball, and everyone in the studio was smiling at the end of the recording session. Same thing for the sessions I did with Elvis Costello and the London Symphony Orchestra at Abbey Road Studios. Simply put: We're lucky.
2. **Listen when you play!** Whether you're playing with a big band, small group, symphony orchestra, or in solo at a drum clinic (and who isn't these days?), the key to a "great" and enjoyable performance is to truly *listen* to the music. That means to hear everything that's there: The sound of your instrument; the sound of the room; the shape or "arc" of the musical phrases; what the ensemble is doing before, during, and after your entrance; relative dynamics; the soloist; and so on. If you stop and think about it, that's a lot of information. My recommendation: Don't stop and think about it. Just concentrate, relax (remember, have fun) and...
3. **Breathe deeply.** Oxygen makes all things possible. I find that breathing deeply helps me to realize and to feel honest gratitude for being able to do what I do—be a musician. Breathing provides fuel to the muscles and clarity to the brain; it also helps to bring awareness of the musical elements into focus.
4. **Tone.** This is the sound of our instruments and ourselves. The aesthetic properties of percussive performance are dependent upon such basic things as the stroke we use when playing. Asking such questions as: How tightly is the stick or mallet being gripped? What kind of rebound is occurring? What is the angle of the stick or mallet in relation to the playing surface of the instrument? These questions and more will then lead the curious drummer to consider...
5. **Touch**, or **articulation.** I will confine this paragraph to a narrow discussion of the concept that a percussion instrument will vibrate or resonate after being struck only as long as the player allows it to. In other words, a drumhead or cymbal will ring freely only until they are struck again (or dampened). This means that the faster you play on your tom-toms or cymbals, the less tone you're apt get out of them. (My college professor, George Gaber, taught me this point.) If you're only interested in speed and density, you can skip this paragraph; otherwise, beware and avoid the seduction to express musical emotions by way of pure velocity and repetition. Allow your instrument, and yourself, to sing. Hey, that takes us back to *listening!* And (musical) *breathing*, too.
6. **Tuning.** First, try to hear the sound in your head (your mind's ear). The style of the music you're playing may well determine the appropriate pitch range and tuning concept to go after. Pay attention to the relative tensioning of each tuning lug with every turn of the key; a drumhead should be in tune with itself, i.e., as evenly tensioned as possible. Avoid extremes in pitch for the easiest tuning. Or, go for extremes in pitch if you're looking for a different sound (for example, an 18" bass drum will sound great tuned wide-open and relatively low in pitch but will also sound really wild if you tighten both heads up extremely high in pitch). Don't be afraid to experiment. A consideration: Sometimes, a taut bass drum or tom-tom tuning can make it a lot easier to articulate on the drumset because of the heightened/speedier rebound. However, avoid having your instrument feel like a Formica tabletop.

7. **Texture.** "Brushes" is the first word that comes to mind. And there are now plenty of interesting brush implements to choose from and use on the kit. Brushes allow the drummer to (easily) play legato. The use of a brush-like tool immediately brings a different textural element to the table. The opportunity to use lateral movement (as opposed to the more traditional straight-up-and-down arc of a drumstick or mallet) brings modern drumming full-circle back to some of its scraping origins. I like to play the brushes. And I really like to listen to such drummers as Jeff Hamilton, Ed Thigpen, Elvin Jones, Steve Gadd, Louie Bellson, Buddy Rich, and Philly Joe Jones play the brushes. All is right with the world. (Go straight back to point number 1!) Also, consider that sticks can also get into the texture game. I often like to play on various parts of the kit, other than the "skins," with my sticks, such as on the rims, shells, cymbal stands, or other pieces of hardware. One of my favorite devices is to place my right stick in-between the two mounted rack toms and play on the surfaces of the drum shells and hardware like they're some sort of triangle. I hold the stick loosely and kind of let it flop around. Sometimes, it's OK to develop your own...
8. **Technique.** Everybody needs it. Technique enables us to play what we hear in our musical head or imagination. The more technique one has, the more things one might be able to do. Real technique, though, might be having all the chops in the world but not really showing them off too much. Musical modesty? It's an aesthetic call. I consider myself as having modest technique, but I was finally able to stop beating myself up about it when I spoke with Freddy Gruber, who surprised me with this observation: "The only bad technique is if you're hurting yourself when you play." I'm still practicing my single and double strokes, and I hope to be able to consistently execute a perfect four-stroke ruff on the snare drum by the time I'm eighty. Meanwhile, the other players in most bands I've worked with are more concerned with...
9. **Time.** To be more specific, I'm referring to what's called the *time feel*. It's the *raison d'être* for our being as drummers. If you stop and think about it, music really is a miracle. Not only does music allow the expression of all that cannot be otherwise expressed, but it flies and soars and depends completely upon the sense of rhythmic movement or velocity as played by the drummer. A good, flowing rhythm with the properly proportioned amount of space between the beats results in music that makes people dance and move and the rest of the band play their best. Bad time is like indigestion, as Papa Jo Jones once said in an interview.
10. **Be professional.** Show up early for any gig and be ready to play before the downbeat. Your equipment should be in proper playing condition. Bring a pencil to rehearsals and recording sessions. And bring a good disposition. While drummers like to steer the bus, nobody likes a grouchy bus driver (or, for that matter, a bus driver who speeds, or goes too slow, or who slams too hard on the brakes, or takes turns too narrowly or wide... you get the idea). Courtesy goes a long way, and it opens your heart to musical possibilities. So does learning to play with your eyes open. Whether in rehearsal or in concert, treat every opportunity to play as a gift and a responsibility. But don't forget to *have fun*.

Hey! The secret to drumming is actually quite simple. It's called *life*.

A Dozen Thoughts

1. The **approach** is key: "Do I want to support the tune?"

   versus

   "Do I want to use this song as a vehicle to show what I can do?"

2. Your **touch** has to always be available (from loud gig to soft).
3. **Compose** the tune as you're playing it.
4. Use **dynamics** within a phrase. Create a shape. (You can also create or enhance the illusion of "feel" by the use of dynamics.)
5. Don't over-prepare your stroke. Play **direct**.
6. Two things to always take with you into a recording studio, or any new project (in addition to your drums and cymbals, of course):

   a. A pencil

   b. A **good attitude**! The job is to not only "play the drums," but to help the artist realize his or her musical dreams for that particular project. If I leave the studio feeling happy about the music, and everyone else in the studio feels good about the day's work, too, then I've done my job.

7. When I was younger, I played as if my life depended on it. Now, I play as if someone else's **life depends on it**.
8. Leave something to the listener's **imagination**.
9. Your musical statements must be **believable**; don't be like an actor who doesn't believe his/her lines, consequently rushing through them.
10. **Exercise:** stretching
    breathing
    clearing the mind
11. **Play what you don't know**.
12. Personally, I've played a couple of good rhythms in the past, but I must reject them in order to **find a purer way of making music**.

CHAPTER 17

AUDIO TRACKS

> *"What we play is life."*
>
> —Louis Armstrong

"Pedagogical"

37

This audio track is the only one with a spoken demonstration. Its concern is the subdivision of the swung eighth-note feel in the simplest of all jazz beats: four quarter notes played on the ride cymbal, with the hi-hat on beats 2 and 4.

The difference between the ride cymbal quarter-note pulse when I'm thinking of the swung eighth-note subdivision as opposed to just thinking of the quarter notes is not so much a difference in feel as it is a difference in style, and one is not necessarily better than the other. The 4/4 pulse, as played without thinking of or "feeling" the swung eighth-note subdivision, is a more traditional ("old school") way of approaching the beat.

Please refer to related text under "Pulse and Subdivisions" in Chapter 2, Function of the Drums.

"But Is It Art?"

38

Sweet Soul

Peter Erskine

BMG-Novus, BVCJ-111

This is from the recording *Sweet Soul*, which was made in 1991. The title is a play on words: "art," as in aesthetics, and my first drum hero, Art Blakey.

The piece is an improvisation that centers around the traditional jazz ride-cymbal pattern, while the bass drum states a "Charleston" motif. The "melody" is played on the snare and toms. In the transcription that appears on the next page, the notes indicated as trills (tr) are played as single-stroke rolls, in which the stroke velocity and dynamics increase and decrease.

But Is It Art?

By Peter Erskine

tr
tr
tr
cresc.
mf

“Straphangin’”

39

An American Diary: The Dreamings

Mike Mainieri

NYC Records, NYC 6026

I recorded this with Mike Mainieri and his group American Diary in the summer of 1996. The piece starts off with the drums suggesting a passing train. The feel of the tune alternates between a 12/8 beat and an uptempo swinging 4/4 (*á la* “So What”). In Mike Mainieri’s words: “The piece is about hopping on that passing train and experiencing ‘the ride itself’ (12/8 to 4/4). The inspiration comes from the movement of the passengers themselves, as they bob and weave in a puppet-like motion.” There are some good examples of interaction (and non-interaction!) between the drums and soloists. And what great soloists: George Garzone on tenor sax, Mike Mainieri on vibes, with Marc Johnson on bass. The drum postscript at the very end was inspired by Roy Haynes. The chart reproduced below is the actual drum part I used at the session.

Reprinted with Permission from NYC Records

"L.A. Stomp"

40

From Kenton to Now

Peter Erskine and Richard Torres

Fuzzy Music, PEPCD003

Saxophonist Richard Torres and I played together in Stan Kenton's band in 1972. The album *From Kenton to Now* was our first opportunity to make music with each other in over twenty years. The tune is based on "I Got Rhythm" chord changes—always a promising format for swinging. I start off playing brushes and switch over to sticks during the piano solo (in the middle of a chorus—*not* necessarily a "no-no"). Pianist Alan Pasqua and bassist Dave Carpenter complete the band. We made the entire album in four hours.

I hope that the drum ideas in both this and the previous selection display some of the possibilities of comping with imagination and clarity, while still swinging. I "trade fours" with Richard and Alan before we take the tune out; Philly Joe Jones and Art Blakey are usually my inspirations for trades such as this (Elvin Jones, too, though that's not so evident on this track).

"Know Where You Are"

41

Music for Large & Small Ensembles

Kenny Wheeler

ECM, 1415/16

Kenny Wheeler is one of music's greatest treasures, whether he's writing or playing the trumpet. Kenny put together this big band as a celebration of his music for a tour of Great Britain in 1990. We recorded this (as part of a brilliant suite of music) on a large film-score soundstage outside of London. Soloists include John Taylor on piano and John Abercrombie on guitar, and the great Dave Holland is playing bass.

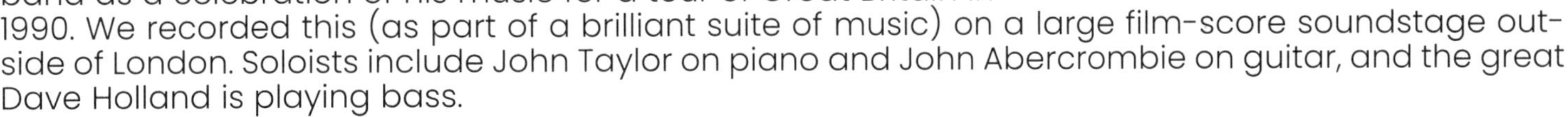

The audio track begins on line two of the drum part, which is reproduced on the following pages. You can hear where I catch some of the band figures (by setting them up or accenting them) while allowing other ones to pass by without comment; sometimes it's refreshing to hear a horn section "pop" a rhythmic figure without the drums doing so in unison. As I mention in Chapter 3, a cool idea is to play the "holes" or "spaces" in the arrangement, i.e., play an accent or figure of your own creation (simple works best) between some of the band's *tutti* statements; you can hear me doing some of that on this track.

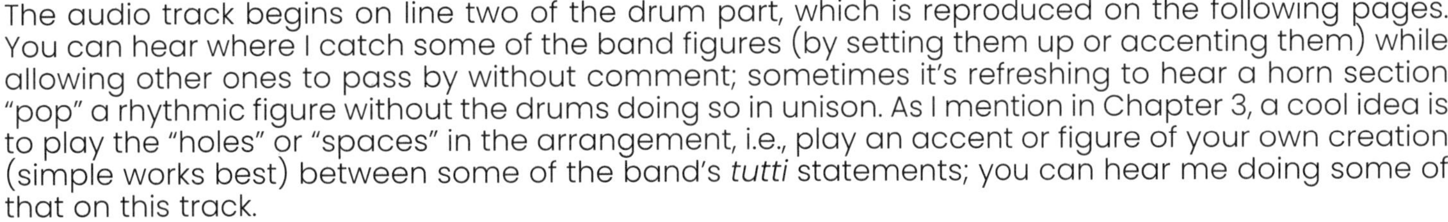

The tune modulates between 4/4 and 3/4, and a metric modulation takes place eight measures before Letter "I"; you can see my notes at the top of the staff, which helped me to switch "mindsets." This is a good example of a drum part that is not too specific in terms of when and where to play accents. When reading a chart like this, your ears are just as important as your eyes!

Know Where You Are

By Kenny Wheeler

Reprinted with Permission from ECM Records

42

"Babe of the Day"

Start Here

Vince Mendoza

Fun House, FHCF-9001

Vince Mendoza has become one of the most admired writers of our time. I am proud to have worked so much with him, and this track is one of our favorites. The drum part is a drummer's dream, as was the band on this recording: bassist Will Lee, guitarist John Scofield, saxophonist Bob Mintzer, pianist Jim Beard. I played drums and tambourine.

Vince writes pretty specific drum parts in terms of which important accents to catch, and I find them very easy to read—in spite of their intrinsic metric difficulties! There are lots of opportunities for rhythmic interplay. I tried to keep the "horizon" of the tune in sight through all of those changing meters. The pattern of rhythm as written by Vince at measures 45–54 and 133–140 is brilliant. We recorded this in New York City, November 13, 1989.

Babe of the Day

DRUMS

By Vince Mendoza

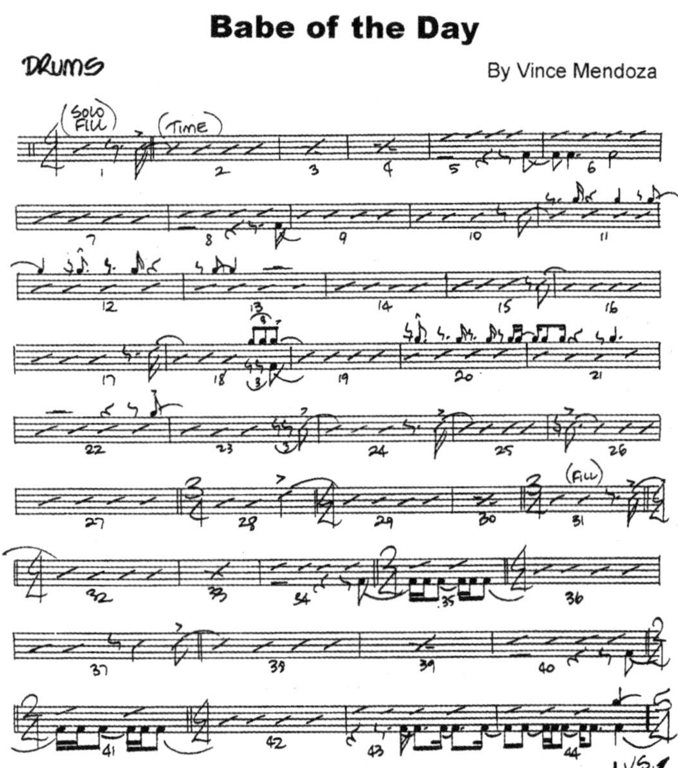

"Not a Word"

43

Motion Poet

Peter Erskine

Denon, CY-72582

I discuss this performance at length in Chapter 4. It might seem ironic or unlikely, but ballads are my favorite tunes to play sometimes. I love the emotive quality of a downbeat and a backbeat played in the "right" spot, with a cymbal splash, low tom-tom accent, or open hi-hat here and there to add elegance and feeling.

Vince Mendoza's arrangement of my composition "Not a Word"—which was originally written as a theme for the Fairy Queen Titania for a theatrical production of Shakespeare's *A Midsummer Night's Dream* in 1987—is performed beautifully by the brass section, and the band of Marc Johnson on bass, John Abercrombie on guitar, Randy Brecker on flugelhorn, and Eliane Elias on piano is perfect.

The original drum chart is reproduced here. Also, see the transcribed drum part in Chapter 4.

"Erskoman"

44

Motion Poet

Peter Erskine

Denon, CY-72582

This tune, which also comes from my score to Shakespeare's *A Midsummer Night's Dream* (the theme for Oberon), is discussed and analyzed in Chapter 11. The musicians on this track (which comes, like "Not a Word," from my album *Motion Poet*, recorded in New York during the spring of 1988, produced by the late Don Grolnick) include guitarist Jeff Mironov, bassist Will Lee, and pianist Jim Beard. The title of the song comes from a moniker given to me by my good friend, director Jack Fletcher.

Note that in m. 70 of the drum chart from the session, where the horns have a "hit" on the second sixteenth note of beat 4, I anticipate the hit on the fourth sixteenth note of beat 3, creating the effect that the band is "answering" me, instead of just playing it as a tutti ensemble figure (as discussed in Chapter 3). The original chart is shown here, and be sure to check out the drum groove and solo transcriptions in Chapter 11.

Erskoman

By Peter Erskine

"Crackdown"

45

Blood on the Floor

Mark-Anthony Turnage

Argo, 455 292-2

In 1996, I had the wonderful opportunity to premiere a piece of music titled *Blood on the Floor*, written by British composer Mark-Anthony Turnage. This movement is an excerpt from the entire sixty-minute-plus work, which was performed by Ensemble Modern (an incredible contemporary music group based in Frankfurt, Germany), with guitarist John Scofield, myself, and saxophonist Martin Robertson as soloists (Martin plays bass clarinet on this piece).

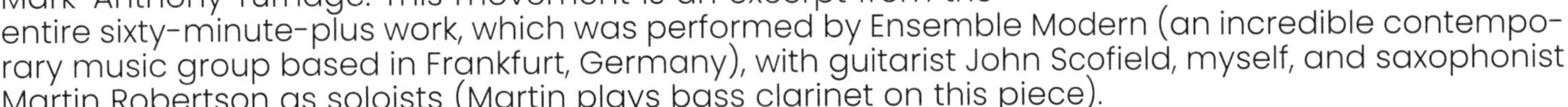

This movement starts and ends with the drums playing solo. I hint at the groove and motifs of the tune in free time, working up to tempo and finally playing a variation of a "second line" drumbeat; John Scofield showed me this particular beat where I play the hi-hat and snare drum simultaneously with my right hand (I hold the right-hand stick in a "backwards" cross-stick grip, more near the middle of the stick's length, so that the butt-end of the stick plays the snare drum while the shoulder of that stick simultaneously plays the edge of the hi-hat) while playing the off-beats (also on the snare) with my left hand. John credits drummer Idris Muhammad with having come up with that; it's very cool!

At first, Mark-Anthony envisioned the piece continuing in the original metric scheme of alternating bars of 4/4, 7/8, 3/4, and 7/8. We convinced him to let us stay in a 4/4 groove after a while! During the end solo, I play with the time in much the same manner as I did in "But Is It Art?"—not expressing the sixteenth notes in "perfect" time, but with more of a stutter. That seems more interesting and emotive to me. (Please see Chapter 14 in which I talk about "Chaos Theory.")

"Crackdown" solo

By Mark-Anthony Turnage

1
♩= 96 "Second-line" feel
*R L R L R L R L R L R L R L R L R L R R L R L L L R L R L R L R L R L R L R L R L R L R L R R L R L R
*Position RH stick to strike snare w/ butt end and HH w/ stick shoulder.
sim.
2
3
3

3
3
3
6
3

4

Freely

p

3 3

3

5 3 6 3 3

6 6 6

3 3 3 3 3

3 3 3 3

3 3 3 3

3 3

rit.

"Elvin's Mambo"

46

The First Decade

Bob Mintzer Big Band

dmp, CD-510

This is a great example of a big band "Latin" chart. Bob Mintzer is one of my favorite musicians and writers, and some of my best memories of living in New York during the 1980s are of playing with his big band. "Elvin's Mambo" is dedicated by Bob to drumming hero Elvin Jones, and the beat I play is a big-band mambo version of Elvin's unique and definitive Afro-Cuban drum gestalt. If you follow along, reading the drum part for this piece (notice I do not play the written/suggested beat!), you can locate the actual transcription examples in the following measures:

- A groove: played in bars 1 and 2, plus throughout solo section (e.g., bars 58 and 59 first time, and 78 and 79 first time).
- B groove: bars 26 and 27 first time.
- A groove variation 1: bars 17 and 18 first time after repeat back to 17.
- A groove variation 2: bars 23 and 24 first time.
- A groove variation 3: bars 23 and 24 first time after repeat back to 17.
- B groove variation 1: bars 26 and 27 second time.
- B groove variation 2: bars 34 and 35 first time.
- B groove variation 3: bars 30 and 31 second time.

The last eighth note of "A groove variation 3: bars 23 and 24 first time after repeat back to 17" is a good example of highlighting an accent on the kit before the band plays its accent on the down-beat. I like to "dance" around a band's figures this way.

Sometimes, the beat I'm playing is the "Elvin" mambo, and other times I concentrate on playing a clear ride bell on every half note for clarity's sake. Note the use of dynamics throughout the band, as well as where and how I'm commenting on the goings-on around me.

The late, great Frank Malabe is playing congas on this recording. His work lives on through his recorded legacy. Phil Markowitz plays piano, and Lincoln Goines is playing bass. I forgot to bring a cowbell to the recording session (!), which took place in New York on September 22–23, 1990. Bob Mintzer plays the tenor solo, and Keith O'Quinn plays the trombone solo.

Elvin's Mambo

By Bob Mintzer

Elvin and Peter, Tokyo, circa 1980

"Elvin's Mambo" grooves

“Not an Exit”

47

Nothing to Hide

Otmaro Ruiz

Periscope/MIDI, Inc., MDCJ-1005

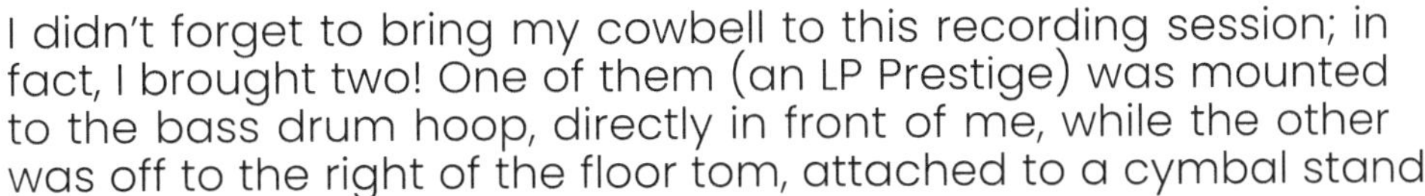
I didn’t forget to bring my cowbell to this recording session; in fact, I brought two! One of them (an LP Prestige) was mounted to the bass drum hoop, directly in front of me, while the other was off to the right of the floor tom, attached to a cymbal stand.

Venezuelan pianist and composer Otmaro Ruiz was a fast-rising star in the Los Angeles music scene; I met him while he was playing with Alex Acuña’s band. In fact, Alex’s and Manolo Badrena’s drumming are the inspiration for much of my playing here, particularly the timbale-like portion of it during the last chorus of my solo. Venezuelan drummer Aaron Serfaty has shown me some authentic things to incorporate into my jazz/Afro-Cuban drumming, too.

A note about the transcription: The solo goes by pretty fast, and the final flurry of notes, transcribed as sixteenth-note groupings of five and six, were obviously not conceived by me to be such exact rhythmic combinations; my intent was to play a timbale-like open roll (or long tone) with a series of accents. For the sake of science, I entered that part of the recorded solo into a sampler and slowed down the playback in order to notate it as accurately as possible for this book. Meanwhile, it’s obvious that I rush the figures at the end of the solo; the transcription reflects the drums playing in time with the hi-hat. As I’ve stated before, the point, ultimately, is to learn by listening. (I hope you enjoy listening to me get excited!)

The drum “part,” like the one for “Straphangin’,” is pretty much a piano lead sheet; on most record dates I have this kind of drum part. I’ll admit, I’m pretty pleased and impressed by my solo on this one. It was a first take, recorded direct-to-two-track in Los Angeles on January 23, 1996. Bob Sheppard plays the tenor sax and the late Dave Carpenter is playing bass.

Not an Exit

By Otmaro Ruiz

ON CUE
B'
F7
Eb+11 7
D ALT
Db+11 7 Dbsus
Db ALT
C+11 7 Csus
C ALT
A'
TACET
DRUMS TACET
FILL

"Not an Exit" solo

By Otmaro Ruiz

rim
*Piano Montuno

48

“November”

November

John Abercrombie, Marc Johnson,
Peter Erskine, with John Surman

ECM, 1502

This piece is an improvisation, recorded in Oslo at Rainbow Studios for ECM in November 1992. The only discussion we had prior to the take was for none of us to worry about where “1” was. John Abercrombie and Marc Johnson are probably two of the most original and creative musicians I’ve known. There’s a lot of nice dialogue going on here. It’s easy to start trying to sound like Jack DeJohnette or Jon Christensen when you’re in Oslo making an ECM album, but I think my performance here owes more to Max Roach, somehow. There’s no transcription here; please just listen to it and enjoy!

49

“Peter at Age Nine”

Summer, 1963; Bloomington, Indiana. My parents drove me all the way from Linwood, New Jersey to Indiana to attend the Stan Kenton National Stage Band Camp. At the final concert of the camp, I played a song with the Stan Kenton Orchestra. Exactly nine years later, I would be Stan’s drummer!

This solo at the end of the song was an impromptu moment, and if you listen carefully, you can hear Stan telling me, “Play, Peter!” Joe Morello’s solo on Dave Brubeck’s recording of “Take Five” is an obvious influence here.

What’s interesting is that no matter what else I’ve learned over the years, I still essentially play and sound quite the same as I did when I was a child—fuel for the “acorn growing into a tree” argument; i.e., we are who and what we are. At least, it’s nice to think that way about the better qualities of our being! Anyway, pardon the indulgence, but I thought the inclusion of this would be entertaining, if not instructive.

YOUNG VIRTUOSO—Peter Erskine, nine-year-old drummer and trumpeter, performed for audiences on Steel Pier with the Stan Kenton orchestra last week, giving evidence that Kenton’s summer music clinics are preparing American youngsters for the day when they’ll hold the future of American jazz. Peter is the son of Dr. and Mrs. Frec Erskine of 1634 Shore Rd., Linwood.

“Peter at Age Nine” solo

"The Eighth Miracle"

Bob Curnow and I go way back to the Stan Kenton Orchestra days when he was an arranger and producer for the band while I was the drummer (1972–75). We even go back further than that to when he was a trombonist in the band and I was a kid drummer sitting in back in 1963. Bob is perhaps best known for his innovative big band arrangements of the music of Pat Metheny and Lyle Mays.

The musicians who played these parts and solos are among the very best in the world: Wayne Bergeron (trumpets), Alex Iles (trombones), Jeff Driskill (saxophones), Tom Ranier (keyboards), Larry Koonse (guitar), Damian Erskine (elec. bass), Brian Kilgore (percussion), Peter Erskine (drums), Cuong Vu (trumpet solo), Bob Sheppard (tenor saxophone solo).

Thank you and have fun!

Full-band version

50

Play-along version (without drums)

51

AFTERWORD
MY PERSPECTIVE

One of the first albums my father got for me when I was six years old was *Movin' In* by the New York studio drummer and percussionist Specs Powell. The next albums were Art Blakey's *Drum Suite* and *Gretsch Night at Birdland*. Soon after, during the summer of 1961, I attended my first summer jazz camp, which was held on the campus of Indiana University, where I met, among others, Louis Hayes and the members of the Cannonball Adderley Sextet. Other mentors at subsequent camps included Donald Byrd, Oliver Nelson, Ron Carter, and Alan Dawson. These four men were my friends as well as my teachers.

Meanwhile, my listening library was brimming with albums by Max Roach, Miles Davis, Sonny Rollins, John Coltrane, Elvin Jones, Jimmy Smith, Charles Mingus, Shirley Scott, Dizzy Gillespie, Roy Haynes, Roland Kirk, Wes Montgomery, Milt Jackson, Duke Ellington, Count Basie, Herbie Hancock, and Thad Jones (in addition to Stan Kenton, Stan Getz, Gene Krupa, Buddy Rich, Dave Brubeck, Gary Burton, Gary McFarland, Cal Tjader, Mike Mainieri—and Leonard Bernstein!).

All to enumerate that my first musical heroes were, and remain, the black artists whose genius developed and produced this unique American art form that would bring the greatest respect and accolades to this country, as well as the greatest joy and meaning to this young drummer. There was never any question in my mind of who created this music; there was only gratitude. And music was the guiding light.

Fast forward: The Selma demonstrations in March of 1965 were broadcast live on television during the day. My mother insisted that I stay home from school in order to bear witness. "Watch this and remember."

My musical education continued apace. My parents sought out the best instruction they could find for me. My father was a psychiatrist who had been a bass player in his youth. "Oh, your daddy's rich, and your ma is good-lookin'." White privilege. I can't count the number of doors that were opened for me. I was fortunate to also have been born with a cheerful heart, and there's no doubt that my enthusiasm matched my gratitude as well as my good manners. What I'm trying to say is that I'm certain that my respect and love for these men was apparent enough to them. Still, the amount of good luck astonishes me, and I've never taken it for granted. Music remained the guiding light.

Racism is a malignant cancer. I fear that too many of us have coasted along for far too long without acknowledging or directly confronting its demoralizing, dehumanizing deadliness. The same must be said for all forms of sex-based discrimination and any forms of violence.

I'm neither a social scientist nor a poet, philosophizer, or pundit. But I am an educator, a father, and musician who owes the language he speaks to the valiant men and women throughout history who spoke their minds and played the truth. Music will always be the guiding light. This is my drum perspective.

PETER ERSKINE

SELECTED DISCOGRAPHY—100 ALBUMS

(36 Essential Albums in Bold)

1973	Birthday in Britain	Stan Kenton
1974	Kenton Plays Chicago	Stan Kenton
1977	New Vintage	Maynard Ferguson
1978	Mr. Gone	Weather Report
1979	**8:30** (Grammy Award)	**Weather Report**
1979	Cables' Vision	George Cables
1979	Michel Colombier	Michel Colombier
1979	**Mingus**	**Joni Mitchell**
1979	Sonic Text	Joe Farrell
1980	**Night Passage**	**Weather Report**
1980	Relaxin' at Camarillo	Joe Henderson
1981	**The Birthday Concert**	**Jaco Pastorius**
1981	Word of Mouth	Jaco Pastorius
1982	**Peter Erskine**	**Peter Erskine**
1982	Weather Report	Weather Report
1983	**Steps Ahead**	**Steps Ahead**
1984	**Modern Times**	**Steps Ahead**
1985	**Bass Desires**	**Marc Johnson**
1985	Current Events	John Abercrombie
1985	**Hearts and Numbers**	**Don Grolnick**
1986	**Magnetic**	**Steps Ahead**
1986	**Transition**	**Peter Erskine**
1987	Guamba	Gary Peacock
1987	John Patitucci	John Patitucci
1987	Second Sight	Marc Johnson (Bass Desires)
1987	Short Stories	Bob Berg
1988	Don't Try This at Home	Michael Brecker
1988	**Motion Poet**	**Peter Erskine**
1988	So Far So Close	Eliane Elias
1988	**Time in Place**	**Mike Stern**
1989	Big Theatre	Peter Erskine

1989	Jigsaw	Mike Stern
1989	John Abercrombie, Marc Johnson & Peter Erskine	John Abercrombie
1989	**Reunion**	**Gary Burton**
1990	**Music for Large and Small Ensembles**	**Kenny Wheeler**
1990	The Widow in the Window	Kenny Wheeler Quintet
1990	Weaver of Dreams	Don Grolnick
1991	A Long Story	Eliane Elias
1991	Open Letter	Ralph Towner
1991	Star	Jan Garbarek, Miroslav Vitous
1991	Sweet Deal	Sadao Watanabe
1992	**Fantasia**	**Eliane Elias**
1992	Jazzpaña	Mendoza/Mardin Project
1992	November	John Abercrombie, John Surman
1992	**Sweet Soul**	**Peter Erskine**
1992	You Never Know	Peter Erskine
1993	Time Being	Peter Erskine
1994	An American Diary	Mike Mainieri
1994	Turnage: Blood on the Floor (Ensemble Modern)	John Scofield, Peter Erskine
1995	Alive in America	Steely Dan
1995	As It Is	Peter Erskine
1995	From Kenton to Now	Peter Erskine, Richard Torres
1995	History of the Drum	Peter Erskine
1998	Lava Jazz	Peter Erskine, Lounge Art Ensemble
1998	Sinatraland	Patrick Williams
1998	The Best of Pino Daniele: Yes I Know My Way	Pino Daniele
1999	Epiphany	Vince Mendoza
1999	Juni	Peter Erskine
2000	**Both Sides Now**	**Joni Mitchell**
2000	Live at Rocco	Peter Erskine, Alan Pasqua
2000	**London Concert**	**Don Grolnick**
2000	Seven Pieces	Lennart Aberg
2000	The Hudson Project	John Abercrombie, Bob Mintzer
2001	The Look of Love	Diana Krall
2002	Badlands	Peter Erskine, Alan Pasqua
2002	Turnage: Fractured Lines (*CONCERTO*)	Leonard Slatkin, BBC Symphony
2004	E_L_B	Peter Erskine, Nguyen Le
2004	Mark-Anthony Turnage/John Scofield: Scorched	Mark-Anthony Turnage
2004	The Girl in the Other Room	Diana Krall

2005	Cologne	Bill Dobbins, John Goldsby
2005	Holding Together	Steps Ahead
2005	My New Old Friend	Alan Pasqua
2005	**Some Skunk Funk** (Grammy Award)	**Randy & Michael Brecker**
2007	Eternal Licks and Grooves	Bob Florence Limited Edition
2007	Standards	Peter Erskine, Alan Pasqua
2007	Worth the Wait	Peter Erskine, Tim Hagans
2008	Blauklang	Vince Mendoza
2008	Dream Flight	Nguyen Le
2009	**The Avatar Sessions: The Music of Tim Hagans**	**Norrbotten Big Band**
2009	**The Trio "Live" @ Charlie O's**	**Peter Erskine, Chuck Berghofer**
2010	Standards: Movie Music, Vol. 2	Peter Erskine, Bob Mintzer
2011	**Music Is Better Than Words**	**Seth MacFarlane**
2011	Canyon Cove	Bob Mintzer
2011	**Joy Luck**	**Peter Erskine New Trio**
2012	Nights on Earth	Vince Mendoza
2014	**Songs from the Movie**	**Mary Chapin Carpenter**
2015	**Home Suite Home**	**Patrick Williams**
2015	**The Legendary Live Tapes**	**Weather Report**
2015	Trio M/E/D	Rita Marcotulli, Palle Danielsson, PE
2016	**All L.A. Band**	**Bob Mintzer Big Band**
2016	**Dr. Um**	**Peter Erskine & the Dr. Um Band**
2016	**As It Was** (Four-CD compilation)	**Peter Erskine Trio**
2017	Second Opinion	Peter Erskine & the Dr. Um Band
2017	**In Praise of Shadows**	**Peter Erskine New Trio**
2017	**Truth, Liberty & Soul**	**Jaco Pastorius**
2018	**On Call**	**Peter Erskine & the Dr. Um Band**
2019	**3 Nights in LA**	**George Garzone, Peter Erskine**
2021	Songs from Home	Seth MacFarlane
2022	**Blue Skies**	**Seth MacFarlane**
2022	**Live in Italy**	**Peter Erskine, Alan Pasqua, Darek Oles**

For a regularly updated list of Peter Erskine's complete discography, visit: https://petererskine.com/discography/.

Other Resources

Videos

1982	Live in Montreal	Jaco Pastorius
1983	Live in Copenhagen	Steps Ahead
1985	Live at the Village Vanguard	John Abercrombie, Michael Brecker
1986	Implosions *(w/ Stanley Clarke, McCoy Tyner, Randy Brecker, Eric Gale, Frank Morgan, Ernie Watts, Roger Kellaway)*	Jazzvisions: Made in America
1989	Everything Is Timekeeping 1+2	Peter Erskine *(instructional)*
1996	Live at JazzBaltica	Peter Erskine Trio
1996	GunSmith Cats *(Japanese Anime series)*	Peter Erskine *(composer)*
2004	Erskine Method for Drumset	Peter Erskine *(instructional)*
2004	Live at the Montreal Jazz Festival	Diana Krall
2006	Some Skunk Funk	Brecker Brothers, WDR Big Band
2007	We Love Ella! A Tribute to the First Lady of Song *(w/ Quincy Jones, Nancy Wilson, Natalie Cole, Stevie Wonder, et al)*	Great Performances (PBS)
2009	Buddy Rich Memorial Concert (2008)	Various Artists
2011	Everything I Know	Peter Erskine *(instructional)*

Bibliography

Drum Concepts and Techniques (w/ Rick Mattingly)	Hal Leonard
The Drum Perspective (w/ Rick Mattingly)	Hal Leonard

For up-to-date information on Peter Erskine's recordings, books, and other activities, visit his website at: https://petererskine.com

Signature Products and Instruments

Peter Erskine Signature Drumsticks (original model)	Vic Firth
Peter Erskine Signature Drumsticks "Ride Stick" model	Vic Firth
Peter Erskine Signature Drumsticks "Big Band" model	Vic Firth
20-inch K Custom "Left Side Ride" cymbal (with 3 rivets)	Zildjian
Peter Erskine Signature MEZZO Snare Drum (6x10 stave)	Tama
Peter Erskine Signature JAZZ Snare Drum	Tama

- Size: 4"x5"x14"
- Shell Material: 4-ply Spruce plus 2-ply Maple = 6-ply 6mm
- Sound Focus Ring only for batter side (Same configuration: 4-ply Spruce plus 2-ply Maple = 6-ply 6mm)
- Bearing Edge: STAR Drum Bearing Edge shape
- Finish: Wood gloss
- Lugs: STAR Tube Lug w/ lug nut
- Hoops: 2.3mm Sound Arc, eight tension rods for top and bottom
- Snare Wires: MS20RL14C
- Strainer/Butt: MLS50A/B
- Washers: Metal and Nylon
- Heads: REMO Coated Ambassador (batter), Ambassador Clear (snare)

The drumset is a jazz instrument, but you can play any style of music on it. The "Jazz Bass" was, in fact, played on more hit pop tunes than you can count; the "Jazz Snare" may enjoy equal legendary status one day. Designed to be reasonable in price without any compromise in its playability or sonic footprint, the Peter Erskine Jazz Snare by Tama is a unique 4.5"x14" drum, made of Spruce and Maple plies with a reinforcing ring on the batter side only. The drum whispers and shouts with brilliant focus and snap. The sensitivity provided by the shallow depth is balanced by the eight-lug design, which allows for a low fundamental body of sound. The drum follows your every command, and will take you to new places, too. Every drummer should have a "Jazz Snare" as part of their collection; the beautiful wood/gloss finish assures comparability with any drumset.